DATE			

PROFESSIONAL ETHICS IN EDUCATION

PROFESSIONAL ETHICS
IN EDUCATION

By

JOHN MARTIN RICH, Ph.D.

The University of Texas at Austin

CHARLES C THOMAS • PUBLISHER

Springfield • Illinois • U.S.A.

Published and Distributed Throughout the World by

CHARLES C THOMAS • PUBLISHER
2600 South First Street
Springfield, Illinois 62717

© *1984 by* JOHN MARTIN RICH

ISBN 0-398-05017-1

Library of Congress Catalog Card Number: 84-2426

With **THOMAS BOOKS** *careful attention is given to all details of manufacturing and design. It is the Publisher's desire to present books that are satisfactory as to their physical qualities and artistic possibilities and appropriate for their particular use.* THOMAS BOOKS *will be true to those laws of quality that assure a good name and good will.*

Printed in the United States of America
SC–R–3

Library of Congress Cataloging in Publication Data

Rich, John Martin.
  Professional ethics in education.

  Includes index.
  1. Teachers, Professional ethics for.   I. Title.
LB1779.R53   1984   174'.9372   84-2426
ISBN 0-398-05017-1

PREFACE

Conduct in many professions is being questioned more greatly today than previously as professionals have been accused of disregarding clients' rights and the public interest. The greater public dissatisfaction and suspicion have led to the appointment of lay investigative bodies to inquire into questionable practices. As these trends continue, the right of a profession to regulate itself is threatened and the profession's status is diminished.

All professions have weaknesses in ethical practice, but some professions have made greater advances than has education. Medical ethics has been of concern since Hippocrates, legal ethics has the greatest enforcement machinery of any profession, and business ethics courses are currently taught in many colleges and universities throughout the country. The study and practice of professional ethics in education cannot match these accomplishments. For education to advance as a profession, far greater attention and concern must be given to professional ethics and its instruction, and adequate mechanisms should be provided for the development, dissemination, interpretation, and enforcement of ethical codes.

The purpose of this book is to survey and assess the principal problems and issues of professional ethics at all levels of education—elementary, secondary, and higher—and to present a position on these issues whenever appropriate. The assessment focuses on the ethical grounds for decision-making and the likely educational consequences of the decisions. This book is intended for educators at all levels—administrators, faculty members, and prospective teachers; it may also be of interest to laypersons who have pronounced concerns about professional ethics.

I am indebted to the University Research Institute for a Faculty Research Assignment award that provided an uninterrupted semester for research and writing. I also wish to thank librarians at the Perry-Castenada Library for use of a study room for two semesters, Mr. Samuel B. Ethridge for valuable information and materials about pertinent NEA activities, Mr. Payne E. L. Thomas of Charles C Thomas, Publisher for his encouragement and conviction of the project's merit, and Ms. Pattie Rose for her excellent typing.

CONTENTS

PROFESSIONAL ETHICS IN EDUCATION

Chapter One

PROFESSIONAL ETHICS: ITS STUDY AND IMPORTANCE

The ethics of professional conduct is more sharply questioned than ever before as professionals have been criticized for disregarding the rights of clients and the public interest. Where formerly the public generally recognized the relative independence of professions and their right to develop and enforce ethical codes, greater public dissatisfaction has increasingly been expressed and lay investigative bodies have been appointed to inquire into questionable practices.

The Federal Truth in Lending Act has informed consumers about their rights; and the Civil Aeronautics Board, the Interstate Commerce Commission, the Federal Trade Commission, and the Office of Consumer Affairs are federal offices empowered to handle diverse consumer grievances. State and local government also provides assistance.

In other areas suspicion of unethical practices remains high. Watergate and Abscam raised the specter of illegal and unethical practices of government officials. Charges of kickbacks and malpractice are hurled at some physicians and surgeons; and it is alleged that some lawyers are trying to monopolize legal services, engage in ambulance-chasing and fee splitting.

In contrast to law and medicine where professional organizations act to assure compliance, university professors are regulated by individual institutions. Classroom teachers are primarily regulated by local school boards, even though the National Education Association has since 1929 promulgated its code of ethics. Most professions show an ethical violation rate of 10–20% of its membership a year and educators are no exception.[1] With the media's effectiveness in disseminating information about abuses and at times sensationalizing them, the public's trust in educational institutions is likely to decline without a more concerted effort to enforce professional ethics.

One of the distinguishing marks of a profession is a code of ethics that is defensible and properly enforced. As the public and its officials perceive that a particular profession is guilty of an unusually high number of violations or is lax in enforcement, public confidence and trust in the profession begins to erode. If violations become too flagrant and widespread, the right

---

1. *Encyclopedia of Education*, s.v. "Code of Ethics."

of a profession to regulate itself is threatened and the profession's status is diminished.

What constitutes cases that violate codes of professional ethics? A secondary school teacher, believing that the school administration was incompetent and the school board was not acting in the best interest of the community, wrote a letter to that effect to the local newspaper in order to inform the public so action could be taken. The school board called the teacher in for a hearing, claimed that the act was unprofessional, and took disciplinary action against the teacher. In the teacher's defense, she claimed she enjoyed freedom of speech and press just as does any other citizen. A case of violating professional ethics or one of exercising First Amendment freedoms?

In a psychological experiment conducted at a university, students were asked to administer electric shocks to subjects, beginning with small voltage and increasing the amount until the subjects cried out in pain. Actually, no electricity was administered, but the students were not so informed. The experiment was designed to see whether the pressure to follow orders of an authority overrode their ethical and humanitarian sense. Was the experiment a violation of professional ethics in terms of canons of research on human subjects, or was it a legitimate experiment in which some deception is necessary for its successful completion?

Consultantships, especially for professors in engineering, business, law, and medicine, have grown rapidly in recent years and are considered by some administrators as a way to keep professors abreast of current practice. The Agriculture Department proposed a list of scientists to review the nation's dietary guidelines.[2] The proposed appointments came under criticism because some individual scientists had consulting ties with food companies; these ties raised questions about their objectivity in dealing with food subjects. Is this a case of professional ethics, or an example of drawing a false inference about the scientists' ability to be objective?

"Sexual harassment" on campuses has received greater publicity in recent years. Are cases of sexual advances between faculty and students a form of sexual harassment? Similarly, sexist remarks? Are such cases violations of professional ethics?

These are just a few of the cases that may raise questions about professional ethics. In this and subsequent chapters, many important issues are explored.

---

2. Professors are taking more consulting jobs, with college approval. *The Wall Street Journal* (March 31, 1983): 1, 14.

A LOOK AHEAD

The first chapter of the book examines the functions of professional ethics, looks at the education profession and criteria of a profession, and assesses the study of professional ethics and its present status.

Next, codes of ethics are examined (samples will be placed in the Appendix). Among the codes scrutinized are those of the National Education Association, American Association of University Professors, and the American Association of School Administrators. Of especial interest are the structural characteristics (e.g., whether the standards are universalized), similarities and differences among the codes, logical consistency, and other features. Subsequent chapters extend the analysis of the codes.

Chapter three explores whether professional ethics is *sui generis* or rests on systems of normative and/or metaethics. Thus the chapter pursues the question of justification and whether ethical codes presuppose universalizable moral principles.

Cases of academic freedom in the classroom, the ethical uses of tests and testing, student dishonesty, the student's freedom to learn, and the student's right to privacy are pursued in chapter four.

The ethics of research in chapter five explores guidelines on research with human subjects, ethical issues in funding research projects, conflicts of interest (e.g., entrepreneur research in genetic biology), secret research in the university, and faculty research with graduate students.

Relations with colleagues and education officials are investigated in terms of ethical issues in recruitment, evaluating colleagues for merit raises and promotion, tenure practices, recommending colleagues for professional offices and other positions, nepotism rules, retirement policies, and ethical issues involving faculty dissent, strikes, and disobedience to institutional policies.

Chapter seven concerns the faculty member's rights and responsibilities as a citizen, community misconduct and the grounds for dismissal, teachers' relations with parents, and the holding of public office.

Findings from previous chapters are brought to bear on chapter eight. Chapter eight evaluates problems of disseminating, implementing and enforcing ethical codes. The chapter closes with specific recommendations for improving policies and practices.

The last chapter reviews and reassesses accomplishments in professional ethics in education, points up persistent weaknesses and recommends needed changes.

THE FUNCTIONS OF PROFESSIONAL ETHICS

If professional ethics is the object of considerable attention, then ostensibly it must have certain vital functions to merit such treatment. By professional ethics is meant "all issues involving ethics and values in the roles of the professions and the conduct of the professions in society."[3] Thus the scope of professional ethics is broad and encompasses an extensive segment of the lives of professionals; it excludes only those acts which are strictly private, and those public acts which are done as a citizen rather than in a professional role. An example in the latter case would be the act of voting for a political candidate, while in the former case doing housework or feeding one's pets would be examples. There is a sphere that is *private*, such as what is done in one's own home. That which is private is intended for or restricted to the use of a particular person, group or class. What is private may become public: a noisy celebration in one's home may become a nuisance and the neighbors may call the police (thereby making it a public act).

Just as some private acts may become public, some secret acts, which generally are thought to be outside the public sphere, may have public consequences as in cases of espionage or embezzlement. Private acts are usually not secret but may be restricted, as social interaction in one's home or at a private party would be restricted to those invited. Secret acts once discovered may not only have public consequences but violate professional ethics in cases of a lawyer or an accountant embezzling funds. Private acts, such as the pregnancy of an unmarried elementary or secondary teacher, may in the eyes of some school boards, raise ethical questions that bear upon professional competence.

Public, as opposed to *private*, is that which has no relation to a particular person or persons, but concerns all members of the community without distinction. Thus a hall is said to be public, not because every member of the community chooses to visit it, but because it is open to any person who chooses to enter. Professional ethics is concerned with public acts by persons in their professional roles that raise ethical issues. And it is also concerned with acts that at one time may have been private or secret and have now either taken on public characteristics or relate directly to one's professional role.

The public nature of a professional role has now been clarified. Let us return to our original question, What are the functions of professional ethics? First of all, an enforced professional code of ethics ensures clients

---

3. Bayles, Michael D.: *Professional Ethics.* Belmont, Wadsworth, 1981, p. 3.

that professional services will be rendered in accordance with reasonably high standards and acceptable moral conduct. This confidence enables the professional to exercise relatively independent judgment in decisions affecting clients.

Second, since the professional is rendering a public service, ethical codes assure the public at large that the professional is serving the public interest and should continue to enjoy public trust, confidence, and support. Although the client's and the public interest may overlap, occasionally they may conflict as when scarce medical resources are provided the client when it may be deemed by an official public organization that the physician should allocate these resources more widely.

A third function is to provide a code of uniform rules and behavioral standards by means of which members of the profession are informed of acceptable behavior in order that their conduct can be properly regulated. Such codes help maintain the integrity of professional organizations (especially if the code is developed by the organization), and protects professionals from falling into disrepute, helps to avoid legal suits, license revocation and the like. It also deters increased government intervention into the profession and a consequent loss of autonomy and self-regulation, tending thereby to less professionalism.

Finally, a code helps demarcate an occupation as possessing one of the hallmarks of a profession. This is especially important for those semi-professions that aspire to full professional stature—they have to take on some of the outward characteristics of the established professions while still maintaining their identity.

THE EDUCATION PROFESSION

Characteristics of a Profession

There are some popular misconceptions about professions that should first be dispelled. Just as a garbage collector prefers to be called a "sanitary engineer" in order to reduce the stigma of his work, many people attempt to dignify their jobs by referring to them as professions. A change of name, however, does not necessarily change status. Along the same lines, it is accepted practice to refer to those who earn their living as athletes as "professional" athletes. The term professional in this case has arisen through popular usage to distinguish the full-time salaried athlete from the amateur or college player; it has little relation (as we shall see) with what is meant by a profession. The term *profession* itself, as Becker has noted, is an honorific title, a term of approbation that is a highly valued collective symbol.[4] The public reacts to the symbol, the symbol is prized, many occupational groups aspire to professional status, and sometimes their practitioners adopt titles ("sanitary engineer") that will increase the status of their work.

In the occupational world, there are unskilled, semiskilled, skilled, semiprofessional, and professional occupations. The terms blue collar and white collar usually represent the skilled and unskilled. Though some of both groups can be found in most all industries, a much higher percentage of blue collar workers are found in the older industries (steel, rubber, automobiles) than in the emerging high-tech industries. Usually the managerial and executive groups in industry and government are not included as white collar but as part of the top administrative personnel of the organizational structure, reserving the designation of "white collar" for middle income personnel who are not in prime decision-making positions.

No single occupational group completely fulfills all the criteria of a profession. The extent to which an occupation fulfills the criteria determines whether it will be considered a profession, semi-profession, or would be classified in one of the other occupational categories mentioned above. Some occupations may exhibit some features of a profession but not other features and therefore may be classified as semiprofessions. For example, if a high degree of autonomy among practitioners is a professional characteristic, nursing and pharmacy fail to fulfill this condition because they are largely delegated responsibility by the medical doctor. There is considerable overlap among various investigators' lists of criteria for a profession.[5]

1. **A high degree of general and systematized knowledge.** Perhaps all occupations, excluding the unskilled, have some form of knowledge and techniques, which, in many cases, may be conveyed orally in face-to-face relationships rather than through the mass media or books. But what is demanded of the novice by most occupations is the acquisition of a set of skills and some rules of thumb by means of which the most essential functions are conducted. Professions, in contrast, possess a base of theoretical knowledge which serves to illuminate practice and provide overarching principles which obviate resort to rule of thumb procedures. The principles must be applicable to

---

4. Becker, Howard S.: The nature of a profession. In Henry, Nelson B. (Ed.): *Education for the Professions* 61st Yearbook, Part II, National Society for the Study of Education. Chicago, University of Chicago Press, 1962, pp. 27–46.

5. Among the different definitions of professions, see: Carr-Saunders, A. M. and Wilson, P. A.: *The Professions.* Oxford, Clarendon, 1933, p. 491; Flexner, Abraham: Is social work a profession? *School and Society, 1*:904, 1915; Barber, Bernard: Some problems in the sociology of the professions. In Lynn, Kenneth S (Ed.): *The Professions in America.* Boston, Houghton, 1965, p. 18; Goode, William: "Professions" and "non-professions." In Vollmer, Howard M. and Mills, Donald L. (Eds.): *Professionalization.* Englewood Cliffs, Prentice, 1966, p. 36.

concrete situations. The professional not only possesses this knowledge but is primarily responsible for creating it. The public must be convinced that the profession has mastery of this knowledge and that it can be used to solve important problems which affect public welfare.

2. A long period of specialized, intellectual training. That a profession rests upon a considerable body of theoretical knowledge that informs practice, renders it obligatory for the student to spend many years in advanced study before being licensed to practice. Other occupations, on the other hand, require either the acquisition of skills through relatively short periods of training combined with an apprenticeship system, or through a limited period of higher education because the limited body of theoretical knowledge and the necessary occupational competencies can be acquired without undergoing advanced study.

3. Practice is essentially intellectual in character. Observations of professions in action reveal that their work is basically of an intellectual nature that demands comprehension and application of principles to diverse situations, problem-solving abilities, the ability to reason logically and draw warranted inferences from ideas, and other intellectual skills. While it is true that architects and surgeons also need certain highly developed physical skills, these physical skills are guided by intellectual processes as to their proper use, and much judgment is required in their employment. Moreover, the basic nature of the architect's and surgeon's practice is intellectual in character, readily drawing upon a broad background of systematic knowledge. In contrast, other occupations which demand well-developed physical skills do not rest these skills upon abstract thought and high-level intellectual operations.

4. Organized to provide a unique social service. The professions, in contrast to other occupational groups, are organized to serve the public welfare as well as to foster their own interests. This means that their services are of considerable value to society and should be organized in such a way that sufficient services of high quality will be available. In fulfilling this criterion, professionals are expected to provide gratis service to the destitute and not to shun their fair share of service to this group; they may also be expected to adjust their fees for other impecunious families. While many professionals may at times fall considerably short of this criterion and act as though they have organized themselves for their own personal advancement and self-aggrandizement, this expectation does help to distinguish professions from other occupational groups. While the pecuniary interests of some professionals may have a high place in their scheme of values, professionals generally expect to be compensated sufficiently to pay the debts incurred through their lengthy period of advanced study and to receive an income proportionate to the importance of the service they render to the public. In actuality, supply and demand may be the greatest influence in the compensation structure.

At times the professional may be expected to risk his or her life or reputation—the physician cannot shrink from entering an epidemic area to treat the sick, the lawyer may be expected to defend the rights of very unpopular figures, and the scientists should publish his findings even though they run counter to prevailing tenets of the scientific community.

Although many occupational groups may directly or indirectly provide a social service, their primary motive is self-interest or pecuniary gain. Industry, while it manufactures ornamental, useful and essential products, is based on profits and economic growth. If the motives of business were essentially social service, there would be far fewer cases of products with built-in obsolescence and poor safety features, dangerous drugs inadequately tested, price-fixing, false and misleading advertisement, and other abuses.[6]

Ideally, a profession should provide a unique service that does not encroach upon other professions or semiprofessions. Lawyers, however, are in competition with accountants on tax work and with banks in drawing up wills. Medical doctors must compete with osteopaths, chiropractors, chiropodists, and faith healers for patients. And it is well known that some parents believe they can do a better job than teachers in educating their children; the emerging home instruction movement is vivid testimony for this conviction. Nevertheless, the uniqueness of the service is only one feature that contributes to professional standing; otherwise librarians, who have scarcely any competition, would more likely be considered professionals rather than semiprofessionals.

5. **Controls standards of entrance and exclusion.** Professions must be able to assure the public that its practitioners are competent if the public is to have confidence in the profession and thereby voluntary grant the needed freedom to exercise professional judgment. As a consequence of the type of knowledge and the years of advanced study required, professions have high entrance standards. They recognize that only a select number of individuals possess the intellectual abilities and personal characteristics which are likely to lead to a successful career. The ratio of those who matriculate to those who finally graduate varies according to the profession. Medical schools, for instance, emphasize selectivity in admissions rather than eliminating candidates after admissions because of high operating costs and the great investment of faculty resources in each candidate. After graduation, in-service programs and competency tests for professional development and the updating of abilities are provided by some professions; however only in recent years,

6. See: Lundberg, Ferdinand: *The Rich and the Super Rich.* New York, Bantam Books, 1969; and Mintz, Morton and Cohen, Jerry S.: *America, Inc.* New York, Dell, 1971.

as in medicine and teaching (at all levels), has considerable effort been made in this area.

6. Enforces a professional code of ethics. A profession exerts control over its members through professional associations which establish standards of practice and ethical canons to be observed. It disciplines those members who violate professional codes. For a serious offense a physician could be discharged from the AMA or the local medical society and have his hospital privileges revoked. An egregious offense may lead to revocation of the license to practice.

It is advisable that a code be established for the profession as a whole unless the tasks among those in the profession are so diverse that a single code would be inapplicable. In the case of engineering, because of its numerous specialties and because it is represented by more than one hundred national associations, considerable difficulty has been encountered in securing agreement on a comprehensive code embracing all engineers.[7] The code, moreover, should be clarified at critical points, not only in terms of the language but by a backlog of important cases.

When professions fail to uphold their code of ethics, various public bodies may seek to gain jurisdiction over the profession to preclude further offenses and to see that the public is adequately protected. Such actions would constitute a serious loss of both prestige and autonomy for a profession. In fact, if abuses were sufficiently widespread and could not be readily ameliorated, it is likely that the occupational group would not very long remain a profession in the eyes of the public.

7. Grants a broad range of autonomy. Since a large amount of esoteric knowledge is found in all professions, the public usually does not consider itself qualified to make judgments about this knowledge and how it should be imparted. But the public, to a certain extent, can evaluate the practices of professionals. The public, in evaluating professional practices, is limited to its comprehension of professional standards and their possible applications.

Occupational groups with the least training are generally given the greatest amount of supervision and direction and the least autonomy in their work; whereas those with higher skills have traditionally been granted more authority over their own work tasks, even though no occupational group is wholly free of supervision and evaluation. There are job situations—such as an automobile assembly-line—where less supervision is given because work tasks are highly routine and mechanical.

Professionals licensed to practice should be capable of utilizing their professional abilities in a range of diverse and complex situations without

---

7. Wagner, H. A.: "Principles of professional conduct in engineering." *The Annals of the American Academy of Political and Social Sciences, 297:* 46–52, 1955.

direct supervision. Without this autonomy, they would be incapable of making judgments and thereby would erode their ability to make decisions. This does not free professionals from evaluation; however, it does leave daily decisions in their hands. In order for the public to grant this measure of autonomy, it is necessary for a profession to uphold high standards of entrance and exclusion and enforce a logical defensible code of professional ethics. If these conditions are not upheld sufficiently, or if the profession is adjudged to be motivated more exclusively by self-aggrandizement, then it is likely that a nonprofessional public body will have to supersede the professional body in exercising control.

Is Education a Profession?

No single profession fulfills all of the criteria of a profession completely and therefore it is a matter of the degree to which an occupational group at any given time actually fulfills the criteria. Consequently, some occupational groups that claim professional status may be semiprofessions (e.g., nursing), while other occupational groups may have become professions only in recent decades (probably secondary teaching), and still others have generally enjoyed professional status for many generations (the ministry).

A number of occupations have been classified as semiprofessions: elementary teaching, nursing, social work, and librarianship. In comparison with professions, the semiprofessions have a shorter training period, there is a less specialized and systematized body of knowledge, and they have less autonomy.[8] Whereas the professions are devoted to the creation and application of knowledge, usually enjoy privileged communication, and often are concerned with matters of life and death, the semiprofessions are more concerned with the communication of knowledge, are not likely to have privileged communication, and even when concerned about life and death, the professionals make the critical decisions and delegate responsibility for their execution to the semiprofessionals. Additionally, the semiprofessional has less autonomy than the professional and is more likely than the professional to use his position as a ladder for promotion into administration.

Looking in turn at each of the criteria of a profession, it is difficult to supply an unequivocal answer to the first criterion as to whether teaching has a high degree of generalized and systematized knowledge of a theoretical nature. A large body of research findings about education has been accumulating for decades, although the quality of research in some cases may not be sufficiently high. Much is known about educational systems and the teaching-

---

8. Etzioni, Amitai (Ed.): *The Semi-Professions and Their Organization.* New York, Free Press, 1969, preface, v.

learning process.[9] Unfortunately, the application of these findings to improve educational practice has generally been disappointing, although recent studies of "effective schools" show promise of bridging the gap and identifying critical variables associated with sound school systems.[10]

In contrast, professors are not usually expected to draw upon educational studies but to have a thorough knowledge of their specialty and observe accepted canons of scholarship. Although some graduate students may be given an opportunity for part-time university teaching, frequently they are not supervised carefully by the faculty and even such experiences are not mandatory to qualify for a university position. Thus the test in higher education is usually the mastery of one's specialty (as indicated by successfully surmounting hurdles in advanced degree programs) rather than knowledge of educational studies. Even where teaching is evaluated for merit raises, the evaluation is usually based on observed performance rather than a demonstrated knowledge of the teaching-learning process. Thus this attitude makes sense if a knowledge of one's subject is sufficient for successful teaching, or teaching is strictly an art, or else the current body of knowledge about teaching is too unreliable to utilize. That the professor has earned a Ph.D. is usually sufficient evidence from the public's viewpoint that the person has a high degree of generalized and systematized knowledge.

Historically, elementary and secondary teaching have not measured up to the second criteria of a profession: a long period of specialized, intellectual training. In 1930, the number of states enforcing the degree requirements for elementary teachers was only two and also a minority (twenty-three) for secondary teachers. Whereas in 1940, a majority of states (forty) enforced the degree requirements for secondary teachers, it was not until 1960 that the majority (forty) was achieved for elementary teachers.[11] Whether teacher education should be extended to a fifth year prior to certification would depend upon the quality of the programs and whether the extension is warranted by the knowledge base. Teacher education programs requiring a fifth year have been tested for nearly fifty years without conclusive results, and today the four-year program is still the norm.

The long period of specialized, intellectual training for careers in university teaching is tied to the rise of the research function in American universities. Early programs in higher education, more limited and restricted

---

9. See: *Encyclopedia of Educational Research*, 5th ed.; and Travers, Robert M. W. (Ed.): *Second Handbook of Research on Teaching.* Chicago, Rand, 1973.

10. Effective schools (special issue), *Educational Researcher, 12:* 1–35, April 1983.

11. Armstrong, W. Earl and Stinnett, T. M.: *A Manual on Certification Requirements for School Personnel in the United States.* Washington, NEA, National Commission of Teacher Education and Professional Standards, 1962, p. 10.

in their functions, scarcely envisioned a place for basic research. American higher education from its inception offered a classical education for the development of the gentleman and for the shaping of character. Vocational preparation was largely the task of apprenticeship programs in the community. Only the professions of law, medicine, and theology, it was believed, merited preparation in higher education.

This pattern was sharply challenged during the latter-half of the nineteenth century by the development of the land grant colleges and by the introduction of the research function in the universities. Germany had made considerable progress in developing graduate education and promoting scientific research, and as word of its accomplishments spread, a number of American students and scholars traveled abroad to study for their Ph.D. degrees. As young American scientists gained inspiration from German universities, they adapted and reformulated these ideals in light of American experience. German methods became wedded to British empiricism in the research activities of American scientists.[12]

Yale awarded the first Ph.D. from an American university in 1861, but it was the Ph.D. program at Johns Hopkins University in the 1870s that best symbolized the German ideal of research. At Hopkins, President Daniel Coit Gilman was prepared to argue in the face of a skeptical audience the utility of pure research, citing many of the new technological inventions that were transforming industry and everyday life as a result of basic research and applied mathematics.[13]

Gilman urged that only students sufficiently prepared to provide the faculty with challenging stimulation be admitted to the program.[14] This shifted the burden found in some of the older colleges where the faculty was expected to take students, some of whom were of unexceptional talents, and stimulate their intellectual and moral development. This ideal of scientific investigation as the chief aim of the university, along with the new attitude toward students, spread in diluted form to other universities and eventually led researchers to deemphasize their teaching role. By the turn of the century the Ph.D. was mandatory for employment in leading institutions. The next step was to insist upon scholarly publication as a requirement for promotion. Thus, by 1910 the "publish or perish" doctrine was installed, and the research emphasis of the university had gained a position of dominance.[15]

The research role continued to grow in the next fifty years in major

---

12. Veysey, Laurence R.: *The Emergence of the American University.* Chicago, University of Chicago Press, 1965, pp. 126–27.

13. Rudolph, Frederick, *The American College and University: A History.* New York, Vintage, 1965, p. 273.

14. Ibid., p. 271.

15. Veysey, *American University,* p. 177.

universities; as a consequence, the university has become more enmeshed in the affairs of the larger society, particularly in the corporate structure and the military-industrial complex. Graduate education itself gradually expanded in the first half of the 1900s. In the 1960s, however, it experienced unprecedented growth in enrollment, graduate degrees awarded, and level of research participation. But in the 1970s with the oversupply of Ph.D.s in the humanities and other fields, selective reduction in enrollment occurred, while the retrenchment of the early 1980s witnessed the elimination of some graduate and undergraduate programs at financially-pressed public and private institutions.

Thus it is generally recognized that professors undergo a long period of specialized, intellectual training, but the quality varies significantly by program and institution. Not only general and specialized accrediting bodies evaluate universities and program areas, but numerous faculty opinion polls that survey the quality of various programs have been a frequent feature of academia for several decades. These polls, though still subject to considerable criticism, inform the academic community and the public of current popular judgments rather than examine more tangible features of institutions as do most accrediting teams.

In many respects teaching fulfills the third criterion that its work is essentially intellectual in character insofar as teaching is involved in transmitting knowledge, dealing with abstractions, solving problems, and reconstructing knowledge. These and other cognitive tasks, though perhaps not all found in a single classroom, are characteristic of teaching as a whole. Of course the public school teacher has other responsibilities: advising students, serving on faculty committees, conferring with parents, participating in workshops, and the like. The professor, though he seldom sees parents, may have research responsibilities, consultantships, and various responsibilities in professional organizations. Not all these activities are strictly intellectual in character but are primarily so.

Limitations in the body of systematized knowledge, as noted above, restrict the intellectual character of educational practice. Moreover, classroom teachers do not always use the knowledge available, either in education or in their specialty. Professors, though usually better prepared in their specialty, seldom utilize findings about effective teaching. Teachers also tend to be guided by what works successfully at the moment rather than be guided by basic principles. This tendency leads to a rule-of-thumb approach that neglects explanatory theory and research findings and places teaching on a level with semiskilled occupations. Thus, as a whole, education as a profession has not used its full potential in fulfilling this criterion.

Does education fulfill the fourth criterion that it provides a unique social service? Perhaps the word "unique" is the troublesome word because few occupations commonly considered professions perform strictly unique services; they sometimes must share or compete for clients with other occupational groups. (This characteristic was indicated earlier in the case of lawyers, doctors, and teachers.) Lack of uniqueness of the service does not in itself preclude the public from treating the occupational group with the respect accorded a profession; moreover, despite partly unsuccessful attempts to restrict competition (especially by the medical and legal professions to restrict competition: in physicians' attempts to exclude osteopaths from hospitals, and lawyers attempts to restrict dissemination of do-it-yourself legal forms and instructions), these activities may only raise public suspicion or temporarily lower the status of the occupational group. It also assumes, probably fallaciously, the majority of the public is informed on these matters. It is more likely that the lay person's judgment about professionalism is usually made by personal contact with members of the occupational group or by informal information supplied by others.

Though librarians provide more of a unique public service than do medical doctors and lawyers, the librarian's service is accorded less status. The status of the service varies during different time periods and in different nations. The status of medicine has risen since the 19th century with the development of modern medical practice and the conquering of many communicable diseases. The prestige ranking of the public school teacher (in a ranking of 90 occupations) rose from 36th in 1947 to 29.5 in 1963; whereas the ranking for college professors remained in eighth place in both years.[16] A Gallup poll attitudinal scale administered annually from 1974 to 1978 showed a steady decline in the public's respect for public schools.[17] A 1979 Gallup poll[18] indicated that the public felt the best way to improve respect for education would be to improve the quality of teachers. Thus the prestige of teachers has fallen because of the public's perception of lower quality rather than a clear expression about the importance of the teacher's services. Still, even in the 1960s when there was less criticism of teacher quality, prestige ratings were not high.

In comparisons of occupational prestige across national boundaries, there was a high degree of agreement (United States, Great Britain, Germany,

---

16. Hodge, Robert W., et al.: Occupational prestige in the United States. In Bendix, R. and Lipset, S. M. (Eds.): *Class, Status and Power,* 2nd ed. New York, Free Press, 1966.

17. Elam, S. M. (Ed.): *A Decade of Gallup Polls of Attitudes Toward Education.* Bloomington, Phi Delta Kappa, 1978, pp. 1–2.

18. Gallup, G. H.: The eleventh annual Gallup poll of the public's attitudes toward the public schools. *Phi Delta Kappan,* 61, 33–45, 1979.

New Zealand, Japan, and the Soviet Union were involved in the study).[19] Teachers occupied virtually the same position in the six countries—slightly above farm owners and operators and slightly below certified public accountants and army officers. It should not be concluded, however, that each nation places the same emphasis on the different status characteristics. In China and Great Britain, kinship is more important than it is in the United States, whereas ethnic characteristics are more important in the United States than in Brazil or France. Formal education is of greater significance in making distinctions in the Netherlands, Germany, and Sweden than in the United States. Less deference is attached to occupation in the United States than in Germany.[20]

But prestige is not the complete picture. Professional service is supposed to display what Parsons calls universalism.[21] A professional is oriented toward clients in terms of general standards. Only in extraoccupational activities can a professional relate to others in terms of *particularism;* i.e., as particular individuals with specific personalities and characteristics that are attractive or unattractive to the professional. Particularistic considerations are out of place in relations with clients. Thus the professional must provide a service to whoever requests it irrespective of age, race, religion, sex, politics, social status, or other characteristics. A nonprofessional, on the other hand, may act on *particularism* and withhold services without, or with minor, censure.

The professional must be prepared to render service upon request, whether convenient or not. Moreover, because one would not be demonstrating full professional competence and also because the service is vital to clients, the professional must always give the highest calibre services possible. In contrast, the nonprofessional can provide an inferior product or service depending upon whether he approves of certain attributes of the customer or else finds it advantageous for pecuniary gain (as in offering products for sale before adequately testing them, or a salesperson's refusal to wait on blacks or Hispanics or deliberately giving them inferior service after a sale because of racial or ethnic prejudice).

To what extent does education as a profession fulfill the fifth criterion of controlling the standards of entrance and exclusion? This is one of the functions that an occupational group must establish early if it aspires to full

19. Inkeles, Alex and Ross, Peter H.: National comparisons of occupational prestige. *American Journal of Sociology, 61:* 329–339, 1956.

20. *Encyclopedia Britannica;* 1960, s.v. Class.

21. Parsons, Talcott and Shils, Edward A. (Eds.): *Toward a General Theory of Action.* New York, Harper Torchbooks, 1951, p. 82.

professional stature. In terms of the temporal sequence for achieving professional status, an occupation group must first recognize common interests that supersede competing interest; maintain standards of performance; and have practitioners control access to the occupation.[22]

Scholastic Aptitude Test (SAT) scores and Graduate Record Examination (GRE) scores are low for prospective teachers. Scores reported in 1980 for college-bound seniors who planned to major in education were some of the lowest on the SAT: verbal 385 and math 418, compared with the national average of verbal 424 and math 466 for students in all fields.[23] Scores of education majors on the GRE have significantly declined since 1970 and are lower than those of majors in eight other professional fields compared in 1975 and 1976.[24]

Changes, however, are underway. Fourteen states required competency tests for teachers in 1980, and bills for similar requirements are under consideration in many other states. The National Council for the Accreditation of Teacher Education (NCATE) denied accreditation to 30 percent of the programs it evaluated as compared to several years earlier where fewer than 10 percent were denied.[25] Although competency tests leave much to be desired, including an accusation that they are biased against minority groups and cannot predict who will become effective teachers, they may at least indicate those who lack a sufficient knowledge base in their subject (if the test is valid and designed for that purpose).

Exclusion of teachers seems to be met more by voluntary terminations and the need to reduce staff (known as "reduction in force") because of declining enrollments or financial exigencies than by dismissal for incompetency. Older people and young women are the two most termination-prone groups, with the older group terminating for health reasons or early retirement and young women leaving to devote more time to their families and frequently seeking to reenter teaching when their children no longer need full-time attention. A greater number of women with families in recent years are not terminating because of the trend to combine marriage with a career.

Dismissal of nontenured teachers, in contrast to tenured teachers, does not usually require due process proceedings. Policies of personal evaluation are determined by the local school board. School boards possess considerable flexibility in devising policies, but must take into consideration federal and

22. Moore, Wilbert E.: *The Professions: Roles and Rules.* New York, Russell Sage, 1970, p. 10.

23. Watkins, B.: Schools of education tightening programs in response to attacks on teacher training. *Chronicle of Higher Education,* 1 & 10, March 2, 1981.

24. Weaver, W. T.: Educators in supply and demand: Effects on quality. *School Review, 86,* 552–593, 1978.

25. Watkins, Schools of education.

state laws, court cases, and collective bargaining agreements. Most school districts have been reluctant to permit teachers to participate in developing personnel evaluation criteria; consequently, many local teacher organizations have sought to place in teacher contracts the right to participate in devising evaluation criteria and procedures.

Tenure is not universally granted in schools and colleges and it is not a constitutionally protected right; yet it is a provision usually adhered to and protected by due process. Grounds for termination of tenure are those of proven incompetence, gross personal misconduct, financial exigency, or program retrenchment. The most common cause in recent years for terminating tenured teachers is financial exigency or program retrenchment. Incompetence is more difficult to establish definitively and many times involves the administration in lengthy hearings.

One characteristic of a profession is that the members themselves establish standards and adjudicate cases. But this is not the case for classroom teachers, as local school boards and state boards of education (other than the state superintendent) are composed entirely of laypersons. Thus in this respect and the lack of rigorous control over entrance and exclusion, teaching at the elementary and secondary levels lacks full professional status.

In higher education, career opportunities have decreased dramatically in the past decade, thereby necessitating Ph.D.s to seek alternative careers and undergo an additional period of career preparation. Only belatedly did graduate schools reduce the overproduction of doctorates. Requirements for employing new faculty have been raised in many colleges and universities during the past decade, including smaller, less well-known colleges and community colleges. The recession and retrenchment in state budgets led to the abolition of certain programs and departments in some state-supported institutions. Shortfalls in state budget appropriations were experienced in Ohio, Illinois, Iowa, Michigan, Washington, Idaho, Oregon, and other states. Since the 1970s a smaller percentage of faculty on probationary status have been granted tenure. Established as a maximum of six years probationary period at any one institution by the American Association of University Professors (as compared generally to three years in the public schools), tenure has been increasingly difficult to secure with the shortage of tenured slots and numerous applicants, especially at recognized universities, ready to fill the place of any professor denied tenure.

Thus the entrance requirements in higher education have become more rigorous in recent years; however, has exclusion been weak because of the security of tenure? Though no doubt true that some mediocrity is shielded by tenure, it is conceded by tenure supporters that this is a small price to pay for the protection of academic freedom. Moreover, this problem, they add, can be avoided by use of adequate screening procedures. Tenured faculty can still be terminated for proven incompetence, gross personal misconduct, financial exigency, or program retrenchment. The control over termination may be jointly supervised by faculty and administration, or in less recognized colleges be the exclusive prerogative of the administration and board of regents.

Two approaches have been used recently to upgrade the quality of tenured faculty: early retirement and faculty development programs. Administrators have expressed concern that the faculty as a whole is growing older and the need for new faculty as a result of rising enrollments may not increase appreciably until the mid or late 1990s (depending upon what set of projections are employed). Thus in order to inject "new blood" into faculties, early retirement is encouraged by some institutions; yet few new plans to make earlier retirement financially feasible have been initiated by colleges or universities. Additionally, pressure for early retirement may engender resentment, alienation, and conflict among older tenured faculty, the administration and untenured faculty.

In addition to salary raises and promotions based on merit plans that usually employ some mix of assessing teaching, research, and service, faculty development programs have been expanded in recent years. These programs attempt to maintain and improve the competence of faculty members in fulfilling their obligations to their employing institutions. Faculty development is sometimes viewed narrowly as the improvement of instructional skills or, in other cases, as the total development of the faculty member. The latter view is obviously more significant for improving higher education but also more difficult to implement successfully.

In summary, though entrance and exclusion criteria exhibit some insitutional variation, generally the degree of their fulfillment in higher education meets professional standards. Special problems, already noted, with the oversupply of Ph.D.s and budgetary retrenchment, need to be successfully addressed if faculty quality is to improve.

Since the sixth criteria—enforces a code of professional ethics—will be discussed at length in subsequent chapters, let us look more closely at the seventh and final criterion: Grants a broad range of autonomy. Through lay state and local boards, state curriculum guides, and the multiplication of bureaucratic rules and regulations, one is lead to believe that teachers have little autonomy. On the other hand, teachers in their self-contained classrooms can, in some instances, close the doors and do what they believe is best. Supervisors and principals seldom visit their classes except during the probationary period, although in other school systems infrequent visits may be made to the classrooms of tenured teachers. Principals frequently require teachers to submit detailed lesson plans, which is an abridgment of the teacher's autonomy. Moreover, even with tenure, some teachers are afraid to discuss controversial issues for fear that an issue may touch a sensitive community nerve. Although the history of academic freedom in public schools is bleak during certain periods, stronger teacher organizations and supportive court decisions have recently afforded greater protection. In conclusion, elementary and secondary teachers do not as yet have the degree of autonomy that is typical of professions.

In viewing autonomy in higher education, a distinction can be made between autonomy of the institution and the professor's autonomy, a distinction that roughly parallels the use of the term in politics as opposed to philosophy. The political use of the term 'autonomy' seldom refers to absolute independence and freedom but is used with reference to states belonging to an empire, a federation, or commonwealth in which autonomy implies independence from the central power only in matters of self-government while recognizing the central government's sovereignty, especially in foreign policy. In contrast, the philosophical usage designates a theoretical or ideal freedom in which the individual is totally self-governing and acknowledges no claim of another to control or interference. The university would usually be considered in the political sense of the term and the professor in the philosophical sense.

In the political sense of autonomy, the university has a relation to governing boards, state government (if a public institution), and accrediting agencies. The professor, on the other hand, may aspire, despite limits on the university, to be autonomous in the philosophical sense.

The university has long struggled for greater independence, from the period of constraints by monarchs and the established church to the modern period of constraint from government agencies and boards of trustees. Greater independence was achieved in American universities by 1950, but this newly-found independence was to be eroded by a series of new forces by 1970.[26] Campus disruptions during the 1960s, the disagreements that arose among faculty, and the erosion of respect for the university led to greater outside control. The needs for specialized high-level skills and practical research stimulated to greater state and federal intervention. As universities became increasingly dependent upon the state for finance, greater controls were exercised by state government. The freedom of university officials and faculty to make unilateral decisions eroded in the areas of academics, programs, research, finance, and judicial matters.[27]

In academic decisions, where faculty at one time made student admission decisions, this function has been delegated to admission officers who, in

---

26. Ross, Murray G.: *The University: The Anatomy of Academe.* New York, McGraw, 1976, pp. 180, 223–25.

27. Corson, John J.: *The Governance of Colleges and Universities* (Rev. ed.). New York, McGraw, 1975, pp. 52–56.

turn, must abide by federal provisions for student financial assistance and state laws that may require all graduates of state high schools to be admitted to public institutions. Where once the faculty and administration made decisions about faculty—hiring, compensation, and tenure—civil service rules and some state legislatures now promulgate regulations.

Similarly, other areas are restricted. State coordinating agencies review and approve programs in public institutions, and programs in both public and private institutions are influenced by accrediting agencies. In research, funds from federal agencies have grown rapidly in recent decades (though declined for some disciplines beginning in the 1970s); federal funds greatly influence the type of research faculty undertake. As for finance, federal regulations concerning Affirmative Action, state coordinating board regulations, shortfalls in state budgets, and many other factors have influenced the university's financial future. Judicial decisions in such areas as conditions of employment, admissions, student discipline, and equal opportunity have circumscribed the independence of universities. Thus at the institutional level the notion of autonomy, even in the political sense of the term, is not fully applicable. What can be seen are areas where university officials can act independently of outside constraints while complying with the regulations and mandates noted above.

The faculty experienced these changes and also witnessed pressures indicated earlier—overproduction of Ph.D.s; administrative policies for earlier retirement; elimination of programs and departments; reductions in annual budgets because of recessionary shortfalls in the state treasury; increased bureaucratic regulations from the administration, state and federal governments. Not surprisingly, the unionization of faculty, especially in smaller colleges, gained momentum during these parlous times. Despite these constraints, academic freedom and tenure, despite newly emerging problems (to be discussed in chapter four), provide professors with a modicum of professional independence and some jurisdiction in decision-making. The philosophical ideal of autonomy, however, is inapplicable to the professor's role in the 1980s except as an unrealistic ideal. Whether sufficient independence is currently granted professors to perform their professional roles adequately is a question which must await an answer after more evidence is provided in subsequent chapters. Professors, however, enjoy a greater degree of autonomy than public school teachers and ministers but probably less than physicians and lawyers in private practice.

Professionalization Reconsidered

Since no occupational group completely fulfills the criteria of a profession previously enumerated, the criteria actually serve as an ideal type or a model of what an occupational group should aim for in seeking professional status. The term 'profession' is also a term of approbation, an honorific title; it serves as a valued symbol. 'Profession' is not a neutral term but what Turner has called a *folk concept*.[28] Such a concept is to be studied by noting its use and the role it serves in society. Such a study, however, may be a difficult undertaking because there may be multiple folk concepts in a complex society as our own. Dingwall claims that it would be better to study how occupational members in their everyday activities define the term profession rather than have sociologists define it by fiat.[29]

Another approach would be to develop a theory of occupations that could be applied to various societies during different time periods.[30] This theory would analyze the historic professions without assuming that professions represent a single, generic type of occupation. It would recognize that professions emerge out of different historical situations and that it would be futile to seek an essence of the professions.

Thus it is true that professions carry varying meanings in different historical periods and cultures. But if professions are to be studied, one has to recognize what organizational patterns to observe; a framework is needed and a flexible theory of occupations might supply it. The social scientist can formulate criteria of a profession or record the distinctions made by professionals in their everyday activities. Why not do both, see where the discrepancies lie, then seek to explain the discrepancies and, if desirable, try to reconcile them.

It has also been suggested that professionalism should be regarded as a scale rather than a cluster of attributes, and that the attributes have differing values.[31] In other words, there are no necessary and sufficient conditions for professions and such a scale would vary by profession, time period, and the particular society. Thus, to take an example, autonomy has traditionally not been deemed important for public school teachers, and its importance for professors was recognized belatedly with the rise of the research university in the late nineteenth century. Autonomy, though actually limited (as noted earlier), is important at all levels but more greatly needed for those involved in discovering new knowledge rather than transmitting existing knowledge. How much autonomy is needed in other professions depends upon their respective goals and role requirements.

---

28. Turner, Ralph H.: The normative coherence of folk concepts. *Research Studies of the State College of Washington, XXV,* 127–36, 1957.

29. Dingwall, R.: Accomplishing professions. *Sociological Review, 24,* 331–49, 1976.

30. Freidson, Eliot: The theory of professions: State of the art. In Dingwall, Robert and Lewis, Philip (Eds): *The Sociology of the Professions: Lawyers, Doctors and Others.* New York, St. Martin's, 1983, pp. 19–37.

31. Moore, *The Professions,* p. 5.

A difference could also be noted between the emergence of a profession and its full recognition. For the former an occupational group would need to begin controlling standards of entrance and exclusion and to formulate a code of ethics. Full recognition can be secured only when more of the criteria are fulfilled to a greater extent, including not only the formulation but the enforcement of a code of ethics. Since an established ethical position and its exemplification in the occupational life of practitioners are vitally important in professional practice, then it would be useful to gain an overview of what the study of professional ethics entails.

THE STUDY OF PROFESSIONAL ETHICS

The professions and professional ethics are more publicized than ever before. Many dramatic cases have come to public attention: Watergate, Abscam, stealing documents for political advantage, lawyers bilking clients, corporate fraud and bribery, physicians defrauding the government by billing Medicare and Medicaid for services not rendered, scientists falsifying research data, professors involved in conflicts of interest between their consulting and extramural activities and their university responsibilities, teachers using the promise of a high grade in a course to make amorous advances with their students, and psychotherapists entering into sexual relations with their clients under the guise that doing so will help alleviate the client's emotional problems.

In addition to their recent notoriety, other reasons can be found for the greater interest in professional ethics. Not only the total number of professionals has increased, but also their percentage in the total population. Society increasingly relies on advanced technology dominated by professionals: the economy is shifting from a labor-intensive heavy industry to a post-industrial society of high technology. Professionals are seen as vital to the nation's future. With greater visibility of professionals, their societal importance, and the fact that they have not always policed their ranks effectively, public criticism has grown.

Many changes have occurred in the professions themselves in the past 25 years. Professional ethics has received greater attention in medicine, law, and business. Case study materials, texts, and even separate courses in professional ethics are offered in some programs. More articles on the topic are featured in scholarly journals, and journals have been initiated which are devoted exclusively to the field, such as the *Business and Professional Ethics Journal.* The field of education, however, has devoted less attention to ethical concerns than some of the other professions. It might be claimed that education has few ethical violations, or that the ethical problems are less complex and more readily resolved. But such implausible claims must first be demonstrated. In any case, no profession can afford to be complacent or negligent in ethical matters.

The study of professional ethics needs to be related carefully to the profession being studied. Although there is overlap, the problems of medicine, law, engineering, and education differ considerably. It will be necessary to examine goals, functions, and roles of the particular profession to understand the grounds of moral claims. In contrast, professionals as citizens share certain moral responsibilities to which they are expected to comply (e.g., obedience to the law, honoring promises, etc). Even here, the picture is complex because there is a place in democratic societies for civil disobedience.

The study of professional ethics cannot be a sufficient condition for impeccable ethical practice, but it can provide a background of knowledge, understanding, and an appreciation for ethical behavior. It needs to study professions in a complex, rapidly changing society and not limit itself to a study of traditional problems which concern mainly professionals themselves. Subsequent chapters will seek to fulfill those objectives. Chapter two begins this process by examining professional codes of ethics.

Chapter Two

CHARACTERISTICS OF PROFESSIONAL ETHICS CODES

A clearly stated and developed code of ethics that is impartially and rigorously enforced is a hallmark of a profession. Professional bodies and organizations, including those in education, have formulated noteworthy ethical codes. These codes, however, differ in content, mode of formulation, and internal structure; an understanding of these differences is necessary in making judgments and evaluations.

The three most salient codes in education are those formulated by the American Association of University Professors (AAUP),[1] the National Education Association (NEA),[2] and the American Association of School Administrators (AASA).[3] The first two codes are concise, while the AASA code fills a book of 68 pages and devotes nearly one-half of the space to implementation measures. Neither of the other two codes has allocated a proportional space to implementation, though the NEA has elaborated on implementation in separate opinions. Let us look first at the content of each of these codes and thereafter examine their structure.

THE CONTENT OF THREE CODES

The AAUP Statement

The AAUP "Statement on Professional Ethics" (see Appendix) consists of two parts: an introduction and a five-part statement. The Introduction highlights a significant difference in the jurisdiction of professional ethics by observing that the academic profession differs from law and medicine (most of whom are in private practice) by leaving to each higher education institution and to faculty ad hoc committees basic decisions about conduct, while standing by to counsel with the administration and faculty and inquire into complaints "when local consideration is impossible or inappropriate." When dismissal procedures are contemplated, the Statement urges observ-

---

1. The American Association of University Professors: Statement on professional ethics. In *Policy Documents and Reports.* Washington, D.C., the Association, 1973, pp. 59–60.

2. National Education Association: Code of ethics of the education profession. In NEA *Handbook 1979–80.* Washington, D.C., the Association, 1979, pp. 285–86.

3. American Association of School Administrators: The AASA Code of Ethics. Washington, D.C., 1966.

ing AAUP directives on freedom and tenure and faculty dismissal. The key point here, at least in comparison to the American Medical Association (AMA) and the American Bar Association (ABA), is that ultimate authority rests with the institution rather than the professional organization. The AAUP, however, does exercise some control in cases of academic freedom and tenure[4] by investigating those institutions where faculty members have lodged with the Association reports of violations of these provisions; wherever the charges are verified and remain uncorrected, the institution (usually its board and/or administration) is subject to censure, the censured institutions are published in the AAUP's official publications, and faculty members are forewarned about these conditions. Still, the Academic Freedom and Tenure statement is as much or more a code for the administration than it is for faculty. Reconsidering our key point, the issue is where primary jurisdiction should lie; however, it is not an issue that can be settled until more knowledge is gained about these codes.

Upholding freedom of inquiry is one of the hallmarks of professional ethics. This principle requires a commitment to the truth and to the development and improvement of scholarly competence. The reasons for these provisions are not spelled out in the Statement; however, the Academic Freedom and Tenure document does provide clarification and support when it states that institutions of higher education are provided for the common good; this good depends upon the search for truth and its dissemination; academic freedom in teaching and research is essential for promoting this good.[5]

Freedom of learning for students is another provision in the Statement. This freedom, however, has not always been observed in the past. Academic freedom, as originally formulated in nineteenth-century German universities, included the freedom of the scholar to teach and conduct research and the freedom of students to learn. However, the way in which academic freedom has, for the most part, been treated since that time (in the United States) has tended to neglect the rights of students in the learning process.

The professor's responsibilities, according to the Statement, are to uphold the student's freedom to learn by observing these practices: he exhibits scholarly standards, shows the student respect and maintains the confidentiality of their relationship, serves as a guide and counselor, and fosters honest academic conduct.

These responsibilities are plausible even though no further explanation and justification are provided in the Statement. Nevertheless, these responsi-

---

4. Academic freedom and tenure: 1940 statement of principles and 1970 interpretive comments. In AAUP *Policy Documents and Reports*, pp. 1–4.

5. Ibid., p. 2.

bilities are also fraught with unanswered questions about the professor's actual duties as guide and counselor, his obligations in evaluating student work, the problems in ascertaining and adjudicating academic honesty, and the extent to which confidentiality would override such other values as the alleged right of university officials, parents, health authorities, or prospective employees to be informed about critical information concerning the student. An examination of these and cognate issues will be made in chapter four.

A third provision in the Statement is the responsibility of faculty members to their colleagues. Thus the professor respects and defends free inquiry and gives due regard to others' opinions by seeking to be objective in professional judgments, and he accepts his responsibilities in faculty governance.

The Statement of "Academic Freedom and Tenure" refers to the professor as "an officer of an educational institution." This means that the AAUP regards governance as a shared activity among faculty, administration, and the board; this interpretation, then, would entail some peculiar rights and responsibilities that may not be found among other professional groups. These concerns will be explored more fully in chapter six.

The penultimate plank states the professor's institutional responsibilities: she observes institutional regulations as long as they do not violate academic freedom, while maintaining the right of criticism; gives due consideration to institutional responsibilities when deciding on work outside the institution; and gives sufficient notice before resigning her post. These provisions need further amplification and will also be analyzed in chapter six.

Finally, the professor has the same rights and obligations as other citizens, except that when he acts as a private person he should make it clear that he does not speak for his institution, and that he seeks to promote conditions of free inquiry and academic freedom.

In evaluating the overall Statement, it could be criticized for being too brief, insufficiently detailed, containing nothing about implementation, and leaving too much for institutional officials to decide. These criticisms may be warranted, although before reaching that conclusion the other AAUP documents may be of use in supplementing, amplifying, and clarifying this Statement. In subsequent chapters some of these documents will be examined.

The NEA Code of Ethics

NEA's "Code of Ethics of the Education Profession" (see Appendix) is divided into two parts: a preamble and the main body, which consists of two principles, each of which is followed by eight rules. The preamble asserts the importance of the pursuit of truth, devotion to excellence, and the cultivation of democratic principles. In fulfilling these goals, freedom to learn and teach and equal educational opportunity must be supported.

The first principle pertains to the teacher's commitment to the student. In contrast to the AAUP Statement, the NEA Code, in terms of its 16 rules, is phrased negatively rather than positively. Some of these "shall nots" prescribe how learning will be conducted: the teacher shall not unreasonably deny to the student different viewpoints or distort subject matter related to the student's progress. In terms of personal relationships with students, the teacher is forbidden to discriminate against any students, prohibited from intentionally disparaging or embarrassing them, expected to protect their health and safety, to avoid using professional relations with students for personal gain, and to maintain confidentiality unless overridden by compelling professional reasons or required by law.

The second principle concerns commitment to the profession. This principle seeks to uphold the profession by raising standards, attracting able candidates, and by not acting in a way to harm the profession. This means that teachers should not engage in the following acts: falsify or misrepresent their professional qualifications or those of others; help unqualified persons to enter teaching or aid the unqualified in the practice of teaching; malign a colleague or violate confidentiality with colleagues (unless required by law or for overriding professional reasons); or accept gifts, favors, or gratuities that may impair professional decisions.

The Code does not address the issue of sanctions and how the Code is to be implemented. Penalties for violating the Code could be expulsion from the NEA; however, the NEA expects its state and local affiliates to act but would also recognize the large responsibility that local schools share in enforcement. Clarification and precise application of the Code have been left to a body of opinion generated over many years by their Committee on Professional Ethics. In subsequent chapters some of these opinions will be examined.

The AASA Code of Ethics

The AASA Code of Ethics contrasts sharply with the AAUP and NEA codes. The AASA Code is a relatively lengthy code (68 pages), far more detailed, that not only lists policies but explains them and provides a section that elaborates provisions for implementation and enforcement. The AASA Code consists of two major parts: part one comprises a preamble, nine policies (equivalent to what other codes refer to as principles), a set of examples illustrating but not limiting the application of the policy, and ending the section with an overview of the provisions; part two comprises nine sections pertaining to the promotion and implementation of standards. Moreover, the "professional school administrator" (which refers in the Code to chief school administrators) are expected to abide by the NEA Code as well as the AASA.

Of the nine "policies," they could be classified into four types: three relate to the responsibilities to the profession; two to the educational system and the local school board; three to the community; and one to professional growth. (There may be some overlap in these policy statements, but these are the primary areas in which responsibility lies.) An example of each category will help make these distinctions clear. In terms of responsibility to the profession, the eighth policy states that the administrator will not permit consideration of private gain to affect his professional responsibilities. An application of the policy is that the administrator does not publicly endorse goods provided for schools by various businesses. An example of a policy toward the educational system and the local board is policy six which charges the school administrator to carry out policies of the local board, state regulations, and to provide professional services to the best of his ability. An application of this policy is that the administrator cannot refuse to execute board policies because they run contrary to his convictions. Policy seven, which states that the school administrator honors public trust above social or economic rewards, is an example of a community policy. An example is that the administrator must never disregard, conceal, or condone dishonesty among a member of his school staff irrespective of the position or popularity of the person. Finally, policy three states the responsibility of the administrator to professional growth by maintaining and contributing, throughout his career, to the growing body of knowledge and skills in his field. An example is that the administrator will attend conferences and other organized learning activities that will contribute to his professional growth.

Part two of the Code seeks to promote and implement the policies. It does this by specifying the organization and functions of state ethics committees, explains the formation and general operations of ad hoc state ethics committees in states where no ethics committees exist, states the organization and functions of the ethics committee, specifies the functions of the executive committee and the executive secretary, clarifies procedures for initiating actions, gives status of judgments rendered by the ethics committees (disciplinary actions, rights of individual members including appeal of decisions). Thus, it should be evident, that the AASA Code specifies implementation and disciplinary procedures where the NEA Code does not, and where the AAUP Statement largely leaves these matters to individual institutions. In defense of the AAUP, it has issued separate statements that say more about implementation than does its Statement on Professional Ethics, but is still less detailed and offers fewer provisions than the AASA Code, mainly because the AAUP views implementation a matter to be determined by local institutions involving the board, administration, and faculty committees.

The provisions and problems of implementation and enforcement will be examined more closely in chapter eight.

THE STRUCTURE OF ETHICAL CODES

By "structure" is meant the basic framework or form that a code takes. All distinctive forms of life have structures which may permit analysis into discrete elements and into their modes of organization within a total form of life. Structures can be found in living organisms, including human beings, in philosophies, religions, ideologies, languages, and other aspects of non-material culture. Structures are structures of systems; these structures function as part of a larger system, and it is the totality of structures that give the system its distinctive functions. The system of traffic signals, for instance, functions to control stop lights; its structure consists of a binary opposition of red and green lights in alternative sequence.

The generic functions of professional ethics codes and professional ethics as a whole were outlined in chapter one. The structure, taken as a whole, should fulfill these functions in differing degrees, depending upon the overall effectiveness of the code. Some general functions that codes serve (in addition to those indicated in chapter one) are to convey the collective wisdom of the profession and to develop esprit de corps among members. This is done, as in both the NEA and AASA Codes, by citing the commitment of the profession to the worth and dignity of each individual and by indicating, in other statements, the importance of the profession and the responsibilities vested in its members by the public. More specific functions in the three codes were indicated in the previous section.

Structures of codes are not identical but should have some generic similarities. What, then, are the discernable structures of professional codes in education? One outward form that a code may take has already been seen in the AASA Code: a preamble; a body, consisting of a basic principle and a set of nonexhaustive illustrations, followed by a second section in several parts on implementation and enforcement. But by structure is meant more than outward form and organization—though these are important ingredients—but the essential building blocks of ethical codes, both universal and optional characteristics.

Ethical codes are based on obligatory statements. Such statements take the form that "It ought to be the case that . . . " For something to be obligatory it must be possible; additionally, what cannot be done without some wrong being done should be avoided. To fail to perform an obligatory act would generally be thought reprehensible (unless there were exonerating reasons). The nature of obligations in professional codes is to impute "unprofessional" behavior each instance that an obligation is unfulfilled (though, once again, this charge may be mitigated by exonerating reasons).

The first feature usually to be discerned are statements of *general objectives* for the codes themselves. The objective of the NEA Code is to maintain the respect and confidence of colleagues, students, parents, and community members by upholding the highest degree of ethical conduct. The AASA Code states in its Preamble that every member of a profession has a responsibility to act professionally. Thus every school administrator has an inescapable obligation to abide by ethical standards of the profession. The promulgation of the Code, then, is designed to promote positive attributes which will serve that end. The AAUP Statement is designed to set forth general standards as a reminder of the obligations to be assumed by all members of the profession.

In addition to general objectives, codes of ethics consist of ideals, principles, standards, rules, and procedures. An *ideal* is an archetypal idea, a standard of beauty, perfection, or excellence; it is a conception of something in its perfection or a standard of perfection; as such, it is not literally attainable. Examples of ideals are found in the NEA Code's Preamble which affirms the worth and dignity of all persons and the devotion to excellence. These are ideals because they have not been attained in any nation and are unlikely to be completely attained; they are, instead, standards of perfection. The AASA Code's Preamble also affirms a commitment to the dignity and worth of each individual. But if an ideal is not literally attainable, what purpose does it serve in ethical codes? It provides ultimate goals and general directions for a profession, gives its members a sense of loyalty to a higher, inspired purpose and serves, along with other aspects of codes, to create an esprit de corps.

Of course if codes consisted only of ideals, they would not be very functional or useful; but ideals have their place when related to the other aspects of professional codes. *Principles* make up another important part of codes. A principle is a general statement which serves as a basis for explaining phenomena or for guiding conduct. The former type is found in scientific inquiry and the latter in systems of ethics and ethical codes. Although spoken of as "policies" in the AASA Code, their nine basic policies are principles. An example is policy six which states that the school administrator faithfully carries out local board policies and state regulations and renders professional service to the best of his ability. This statement of principle consists of three parts and could actually have been made into three principles except that one principle is more economical and probably more functional. In contrast to ideals, principles state what is believed to be attainable.

A *standard* is a measure established by authority for determining quantity, extent, value, or quality of a thing or process. Standards enable observers to determine whether behavior of professionals comply with professional codes. Whenever standards are used for evaluative purposes, two general processes are grading and ranking.[6] In grading, one decides if something is good or bad, desirable or undesirable; in ranking, one decides whether something is as good or bad as another thing, and sometimes whether it is the best or worst of a group. In grading or ranking, one is classifying educational phenomena according to their worth or value, determined by the degree to which phenomena meet the standards adopted.

In making an evaluation one takes a point of view; and with each point of view different standards are used. One may take an ethical, economic, aesthetic, or utility (feasibility, efficaciousness) point of view. With a professional code, however, the ethical point of view is the overriding and prevailing one.

Standards can take either a quantitative or qualitative form. If they are expressed quantitatively the procedures for measurement are understood, and practices are easier to evaluate. Teacher-pupil ratios and compulsory school attendance provisions are expressed quantitatively. Some standards are qualitative either because they are not susceptible to precise measurement or because it is desirable that they be flexibly adaptable to diverse situations. An example of a quantitative standard is that the state ethics committee, according to the AASA Code, should consist of five members serving five-year overlapping terms. To evaluate the standard one would grade rather than rank, as either the Committee fulfills these conditions or it does not do so. The AAUP Statement, in contrast, provides a qualitative standard when it expects professors to devote their energies to developing and improving their scholarly competence. No matter how many quantitative standards can be found in a code, the overall evaluation of a professional's ethics is a qualitative judgment that may be made on the basis of assessing compliance or lack of compliance with both qualitative and quantitative standards.

So far standards have been viewed from the standpoint of grading; rankings, however, may also be used with standards. When awards are given for professional achievement and service, those who not only comply with their code of ethics but who are adjudged as having exemplary ethical behavior may likely receive the awards, especially when the behavior is combined with notable contributions to the discipline. As such, comparisons are made among nominees and final rankings of the nominees determine award recipients.

Rules are also found in codes of ethics. A rule is a type of generalization used to prescribe conduct, action, or usage. By following a rule one's action is said to be rule-governed. A rule may provide general instructions as to what one should do in order to fulfill an objective. There are numerous rules that provide general instructions: rules of chess, cooking, sewing,

---

6. Taylor, Paul W.: *Normative Discourse.* Englewood Cliffs, N.J., 1961, ch. 1.

driving a car, and so forth. Other rules regulate one's relations to persons or property: for example, rules regulating lining up to receive instructions, running in the hall, walking on the grass.

Rules can be stated positively or negatively and are usually stated in the imperative mood ("Grades in each course are due 48 hours after the final exam" or "No running in the halls"). The NEA Code presents 16 rules stated negatively in the imperative mood, ranging from "Shall not unreasonably deny the student access to varying points of view" to "Shall not misrepresent his/her professional qualifications."

In contrast to standards which can be ranked and graded, rules can only be graded. This means that one either fulfills a rule or does not. Two acts, according to a rule, may both be right, both be wrong, or one right and the other wrong. Some acts are neither right nor wrong because they do not fall under the rule. This is a reminder as well that not only the behavior may not be covered by a particular rule but by any of the rules in a given code. Thus there usually are large areas of professional behavior that remain unregulated by codes and thereby are left up to the discretion of professionals themselves.

A distinction can be made between regulative and constitutive rules.[7] Regulative rules regulate antecedent or independently existing forms of behavior. Constitutive rules not only regulate but create or define new forms of behavior. Etiquette, for instance, is a system of regulative rules; whereas sports and games, such as football, are based on constitutive rules because the rules make their playing possible. In other words, constitutive rules create the game, whereas regulative rules control preexisting forms of behavior. Regulative rules generally take the form, "One ought to do X in circumstances C." In contrast, constitutive rules take the form, "X counts as Y." Many of the rules in the NEA Code are regulative insofar as they control preexisting forms of behavior (e.g., the rule that states that teachers shall not unreasonably restrain students from independent action in pursuing learning). Constitutive rules would pertain to the AAUP Statement about freedom of inquiry, the community of scholars, and confidentiality; as these unique relations are created by the code, and are not found in the larger society.

Another feature of professional codes is *procedures.* A procedure outlines a particular course of action or a method of conducting business affairs. Procedures sometimes provide a series of steps followed in a regular, definite order. Since the AASA Code contains provisions for implementation and enforcement, many procedures are outlined. For instance, it reports the procedures to be followed by the president of the state administrators association in conducting the state ethics committee, and outlines procedures for the AASA executive secretary in those states where no ethics committee has

---

7. Searle, John: *Speech Acts.* Cambridge, Cambridge University Press, 1969, pp. 33–42.

been formed. What procedures should be used would depend upon the given code and their effectiveness in achieving objectives. Not all codes, however, may include procedures; and it is possible that some codes may not include some of the other structural features previously discussed.

To summarize, it was shown that professional codes of ethics may contain ideals, objectives, principles, standards, rules and procedures. Are all of these structural features necessary before a document can rightfully be considered a professional code, or are some of them or most of them optional? If someone should say that *C* is a code but *C* has none of these features, it is highly doubtful that it could actually serve as a professional code; in other words, someone could contend that it is a code but it would not resemble one and, for that reason, unlikely be accepted as such. More importantly, it could not function as a code because it would lack obligatory statements and a normative framework by means of which action could be clearly directed and responsibility accurately assessed. This does not mean, however, that all codes must have each of the above features in order to function as a code. Though each structural feature, as earlier indicated, serves one or more functions, ideals and procedures are the two features that might be dispensed with without seriously impairing a code. Since ideals promote a lofty vision and esprit de corps, a profession may use other means to fulfill these ends. Procedures, especially those which include guidelines for implementation and enforcement, could be placed in other documents or, as in the case of the AAUP, left mainly to employing institutions.

Who is the client of the codes? A physician's client is his patient; in turn, is the teacher's client the student? The answer is ambiguous. On the one hand, the teacher's responsibility is to the student; however, there may be other clients: colleagues, administration, school board, parents, and the larger public. With professors, parents play a minor role, but the professors may have responsibilities to outside sources for funded research, to clients in consulting work, and to one's discipline as it is organized professionally. If by client is meant someone under the protection of another, then clearly the teacher's *in loco parentis* role in the early grades designates the student as client; but if client means a person who engages the professional advice or services of another, then a case could be made for these multiple clients and varying degrees and parameters of responsibility. The point here is that multiple clients complicate sorting out responsibilities and often lead to conflicts of interest (as, for instance, the amount and type of consulting a professor can do and still properly fulfill her university commitments). An effective code sorts out these responsibilities so that the professional's responsibilities are clear. A professional organization may not rely entirely on its code to perform all these complex functions but may supplement it with a body of opinion and interpretation (NEA) or additional clarifying documents (AAUP). But if a professional code cannot be justified, there would seem to be no grounds for the members to observe it. Thus the next chapter deals with vital questions about justification in both professional codes and professional ethics as a whole. Different approaches to justification will be explored and plausible ones identified; the grounds for accepting or rejecting an approach will be developed.

Chapter Three

THE JUSTIFICATION OF PROFESSIONAL ETHICS

Professionals have no cause for abiding by ethical codes and observing ethical behavior in professional relationships unless warranted reasons can be adduced for doing so. These reasons (including pertinent evidence), when gathered together, lead to different forms of justification. When professional ethics has warranted justification, it is thereby grounded and offers practitioners rational and supportable reasons for abiding by it.

This chapter will examine different forms of justification in professional ethics by first looking more closely at its language, the language of responsibility, in order to observe its characteristics and what it entails. Next, the question, Is professional ethics *sui generis* or does it rest on legal systems, normative ethics, or metaethics? is a key one because it delineates the relationship of professional ethics to a larger public morality to ascertain its degree of independence or to uncover whether it may already be grounded in a public morality. Then, different forms of justification are explored and the most plausible and compelling ones are identified. Finally, explored is the question, Who should make decisions about professional ethics?

THE LANGUAGE OF PROFESSIONAL ETHICS

The language of professionalism is the language of both rights and responsibility; whereas the language of professional ethics is that of responsibility. Professional organizations, such as the NEA[1] and AAUP[2], have issued statements about rights. The AAUP's statement is designed to promote public understanding and protect academic freedom and tenure, including necessary measures to assure these ends. The NEA's "Bill of Teacher Rights" is designed to uphold teacher's rights as professionals, employees, and rights of professionals in their organizational roles.

The language of professionalism is unified in the many cases where rights and responsibilities are correlated. If a person has a right to act, others have a duty not to restrain that person; if someone has a duty not to act, however,

---

1. National Education Association: Bill of teacher rights. In NEA *Handbook, 1979–80.* Washington, D.C., The Association, 1979, pp. 283–84.

2. The American Association of University Professors: "Academic Freedom and Tenure." In *Policy Documents and Reports.* Washington, D.C., The Association, 1973, pp. 1–4.

others have a right not to be affected by that person's actions. A simple correlation between rights and responsibilities cannot always be claimed, however, and there is no logical necessary connection between the two. A chairperson may be said to have the duty of presiding at all meetings of an organization, but it would be misleading to assume that the members have the right to have him or her preside. Young children and animals are said to have certain rights, but because of their helpless and dependent state, they are not expected to have correlative responsibilities. Among adults responsibility is more pervasive than rights because one can have duties, responsibilities, and obligations without correlative rights. This is evident in numerous responsibilities of family life, profession, and citizenship.

Rights claims involve an adversarial relationship (someone is denying one's rights); responsibility does not involve such relationships. With rights, a basic equality may be assumed insofar as there are certain basic rights all enjoy; whereas with responsibility, an inequality may antecedently exist in the relationship insofar as needs are concerned (as between parent and child).

The actual language of responsibility is that of obligation (as discussed in the previous chapter), though not always framed in the imperative mood. Conceptually, an active, positive feature of responsibility is that of accountability. Elected officials are expected to be accountable to their constituents; there also are governmental checks and balances; judicial and administrative reviews. The more general meaning of accountability (in contrast to its form in education) is to entrust something to someone and to call upon the person to render an account of how that trust has been executed.

Another positive feature of one who acts responsibly is that he or she uses discretion, assesses the consequences of actions, and tries to act rationally. Furthermore, this requires the ability to make intelligent moral judgments, otherwise one would not know whether he or she was acting responsibly. There are times, of course, when acting responsibly means fulfilling one's duties and obligations, yet responsibility in its widest sense is more than this because it is possible to fulfill duties by following orders (assuming the orders are warranted) and thereby not be required to exercise the rational and moral abilities previously mentioned. To act responsibly may mean to comply with duties, but in many cases it also involves much more than this. One needs to understand the moral features of an act in order to act responsibly. Those whose acts are usually responsible are characterized as responsible persons.

The moral features of responsibility can better be discerned when responsibility is considered a form of responding to others and caring about them. We are responsible only when we are able to respond to others positively rather than opposing, harming, or shirking our obligations. As Dewey noted: "One is held responsible in order that he may *become* responsible, that is, responsive to the needs and claims of others, to the obligations implicit in his position."[3] One shows care and concern for others by treating them as persons for whom one's acts have an effect or for whom others depend for the performance of one's duties. Thus offspring depend upon parents, students upon teachers, and patients upon doctors. The type of dependency that is legitimated and the form that care takes may be socially, legally, or professionally defined. A generally responsible person who fails to respond in a given instance by showing care and concern is likely to suffer remorse, guilt, or inner moral conflict.

Responsibility can be either individual or collective. Individual responsibility, the more commonly recognized type, is the ascription of sole or primary responsibility for an act or related series of acts to one person. For instance, an individual is said to be responsible for paying debts, keeping promises, disciplining his or her children, and the like. In contrast, collective responsibility is the ascription of responsibility to a group, organization, firm, or governing body for an act or related series of acts which affect an individual or individuals, groups and, in some cases, society as a whole. The responsibilities of business firms are regulated by government; governmental bodies by courts and constitutions; and organizations by charters and government. In education, organized teacher strikes and sanctions, school board policy decisions, state and federal education legislation are just a few examples of collective responsibility.

The ascription of responsibility for acts brings predictability into interpersonal relations; it also provides some assurance that fairness and respect for persons will be upheld. Responsibility, when mandated through institutional policies and standards, also reinforces greater predictability in human relations by publicly stating the types of activities that will be tolerated, how liability will be assessed, and the nature and types of punishments to be meted out.

Thus considerations of various forms of responsibility undergird professional ethics; and although responsibility is usually addressed to the individual practitioner, it can at times refer to acts of professional organizations, boards, commissions, and ad hoc bodies. The collective form of responsibility may arise, for instance, where the local professional association urges teachers to go on strike even though the strike itself is a violation of legal statutes affecting public employees, or where a school administration is faced with charges of discrimination in the assignment of minority teachers.

---

3. Dewey, John: Theory of the Moral Life. New York, Holt, 1960, p. 170.

PROFESSIONAL ETHICS:
DEPENDENT, INTERDEPENDENT, OR INDEPENDENT?

Though the language of professional ethics helps us to understand the network of relationships and the normative form of life it entails, it nonetheless only shows that such forms and relationships exist and may serve functional purposes; it does not, however, develop a grounding for professional ethics. In other words, if professional ethics cannot be adequately justified, then the specialized language could be ignored as a quaint vestige of obsolescent forms and attitudes.

But how can such justification be demonstrated? One way would be to ascertain whether professional ethics is dependent, interdependent, or independent of some separate moral and/or legal systems. Thus if professional ethics is dependent, it may rest upon a legal system or normative ethics or metaethics. To say that something is *dependent* upon something else suggests that it is subordinate, that it relies on another for support, subject to another's rule, determined or conditioned by another (contingent), or cannot exist or come into existence by itself.

Frankena's discussion of whether morality is dependent upon religion is useful here.[4] He investigates whether morality is historically, psychologically, or logically dependent upon religion. The same could be done in exploring the relationship between professional ethics and some external system(s).

But before discussing the matter of dependency, law, normative ethics, and metaethics will be defined. A legal system is a network established for enforcing the laws. Laws have coercive power and are an exercise of force by duly constituted authorities through the use of sanctions. Yet this conception of law does not explain the nature of laws which confer powers (such as the making of a will) and cannot be seen as imposing duties. According to Hart[5], a legal system consists of primary and secondary rules. Primary rules impose duties and secondary rules confer powers. Primary rules are the ones commonly equated with laws, such as those regulating property and persons. Secondary rules are rules about rules: they provide procedures for creating, modifying, and abrogating primary rules.

Normative ethics is a study of human conduct: it prescribes what one should do and how one should act based on moral principles; and it provides systems to follow which constitute a moral way of life (e.g., Christian ethics,

---

4. Frankena, William K.: Public education and the good life. *Harvard Educational Review*, 31, 413–426, Fall 1961.

5. Hart, H. L. A.: *The Concept of Law.* New York, Oxford, 1961.

Confucianism, Stoicism, Epicureanism, Utilitarianism, Aristotelian ethics, Kantian ethics, etc.). Metaethics studies the nature of ethics in terms of its language, forms of reasoning, and how moral decisions are justified. It raises such questions as what is the difference between such terms as "good," "right," and "ought"; it develops theories about the nature of ethics; and it attempts to determine what sorts of tests, if any, could be used to justify ethical statements.

Returning to our exploration of law and professional ethics, in the school of legal philosophy known as positivism, law and morality are severed. Thus if one accepts this school of thought, the connection between law and professional ethics is tenuous indeed. Recalling that professional ethics encompasses all issues of ethics and values in professional roles and the conduct of professionals in society, then law does not connect directly to professional ethics. Legal science, according to the Austrian legal philosopher, Hans Kelsen[6], is a descriptive science, and valuational questions cannot be scientific. He therefore posits a sharp separation between "is" and "ought" questions, believes that questions of justice cannot be answered by means of rationality but that value questions rest upon intuitions.

Not all jurists and legal philosophers accept positivism, however. Besides neo-Thomist jurists, Lon Fuller has criticized positivism.[7] Fuller emphasizes the purposive element in the law and only those rules which serve human purposes of furthering certain basic values can be counted as law. The overlap between law and morality can be seen by considering the conditions which a legal system must fulfill in order to regulate social life. He believes that the conditions necessary for such regulation are attributes of the concept of justice; therefore law exhibits a necessary connection with minimal notions of justice.

Turning now to three forms of dependency—historical, psychological, and logical—the relationship between professional ethics and the law is unclear because of the different schools of legal thought. If analytical positivism is accepted, there would be no direct historical or logical connection between law and professional ethics. But there still may be a psychological connection in the sense that before a professional will follow a code of ethics laws must be ratified and enforced that coerce or compel him to act on the professional code. This contention, however, is implausible and unconvincing because most parts of such codes do not fall under a covering law. It is true that certain cases of academic freedom and tenure and student rights (in relation to faculty and administration) have been adjudicated in courts; most of

6. Kelsen, Hans: *What Is Justice?* Berkeley, University of California Press, 1957.

7. Fuller, Lon: *The Morality of Law.* New Haven, Yale, 1964.

these rights, however, did not originate in the courts and therefore do not show historical dependence on the legal system. Thus from the viewpoint of legal positivism, professional ethics is basically independent of the legal system.

Yet if Lon Fuller's position is substituted for positivism, the picture changes considerably. That law is purposive and has a connection with justice means that, first of all, to the extent that professional ethics depends in some way on justice—presupposes it, uses it in adjudicating disputes, or emerges from such a concept—professional ethics is based in some way on legal systems. But even for the moment if such a relationship with justice is assumed, it is not historically evident that concepts of justice originated in legal systems; more likely they arose through negotiation in everyday social interaction, were eventually formalized in customs which became unwritten moral codes and later were adopted and reformulated in emerging legal systems.

It is also unclear that professional ethics is logically dependent upon legal systems if by logical dependence is meant that legal premises are required to justify statements about one's professional responsibilities. How this could be shown is puzzling; but perhaps a theory of justice (such as Rawls) could be shown to have a logically necessary connection with law; then from the fundamental premises of the theory, professional responsibilities could be derived. No one, to my knowledge, has done this and therefore logical dependence has not been demonstrated.

Psychological dependence could be shown if professional ethics is observed because a theory of justice, which has a logically necessary connection with law, serve as motivating reasons for compliance. Even then, professional ethics would likely be only partly dependent because professional self interest, professional pride, and other reasons would also likely motivate compliance.

Metaethics might be used to sort out some of the conceptual problems in ethical codes and to provide systems of justification. But though these contributions may prove important, they still do not demonstrate that professional ethics is derived from metaethics. Does professional ethics depend upon metaethics in an historical, psychological, or logical way? Metaethics, at least as it has developed into competing schools of thought (naturalism, intuitionism, emotivism, etc.), is more of a twentieth century phenomenon; and since professional ethics antedates this century, it would not in that sense rest on metaethics. But metaethics has actually been around since Plato and Aristotle, though not in a self-conscious schools or systems found in the contemporary period. And since the Oath of Hippocrates for medical practice was originated in ancient times (estimates of its actual date of origin vary from the sixth century B.C. to the first century A.D.), could it and subsequent codes have been derived from metaethics? No historical evidence exists to support this claim; in fact, normative ethics, which prescribes right conduct and the good life, is more closely analogous in form and structure to professional ethics than is metaethics.

As for psychological and logical dependency, professional ethics cannot be said to be psychologically dependent because metaethics does not serve to motivate action—this is not its function. Judging from codes of professional ethics, committee opinions supporting the codes, and commentaries on the codes, metaethics was not the basis for deriving the codes; moreover, those who formulate codes do not show any familiarity with metaethics (though some participants may be knowledgeable in metaethics but see no way to relate it to professional ethics and therefore remain silent about it). In any case, deriving professional ethics from metaethics seems highly implausible. What is more likely possible is to employ some metaethical system to justify a code after it is adopted. In other words, if a professional asks why he or she should obey a code on a particular point, say in the matter of confidentiality or conflict of interest, a board of adjudication may give a simple reason such as failure to comply sets a bad example for other professionals or has untoward consequences with clients; but the board might use a more elaborate form of justification by appealing to a theory of justice. It may also be the case that a professional code is more compatible in form with some metaethical systems than others, but this compatibility is after the fact (not because one was derived from another) and may merely show that there are a limited number of ways to formulate codes; the compatibility may not carry any logical force insofar as to think and operate with the code means one must first think in terms of the metaethical system.

Historically, normative ethics antedates professional ethics insofar as various everyday mores and obligations were eventually formulated into normative ethical systems, whether secular or religious. These mores could be found in Hebraic, Christian, and Confucian ethics, Stoicism, and Epicureanism. But to assume because of this historical condition the earliest development caused the later development is the fallacy of *post hoc ergo propter hoc:* a fallacy of false cause that concludes one event is the cause of another event because it preceded in time (e.g., seeing a black cat and then slipping and twisting one's ankle). Even if it could be shown that certain aspects of professional ethics are an outgrowth of normative ethics, it does not follow that professional ethics is strictly dependent on normative ethics. Since history happens only once, a single incident does not prove a necessary connection (it could have arisen in another way).

Does professional ethics rest upon normative ethics, then, in a psychological or motivational sense? This would mean that every time the professional abided by professional codes, the motivating reason was based upon adherence to normative ethics. According to this position, unprofessional behavior is likely to be rife if professionals do not subscribe to a pertinent system of normative ethics. It may be that some people will only act professionally unless they first adopt principles of normative ethics. For example, if truth-telling originated in normative ethics, a professional may need to subscribe to truthtelling as it applies to general citizenship responsibilities before one can adequately deal with this principle in professional ethics. But can it be said that no one will act professionally or avoid unprofessional behavior without first subscribing to a system of normative ethics? Unless there was an isomorphism between normative and professional ethics or a way of logically inferring the latter from the former, this claim is implausible. Certain areas of professional ethics—advertising, freedom of inquiry, confidentiality—do not have an exact counterpart in normative ethics and consequently a knowledge of normative ethics would not provide a sufficient knowledge or understanding of professional ethics. This can be seen in the treatment of confidentiality in the American Bar Association's new code of ethics.[8] The new codes says that a lawyer should inform on a client only when silence could lead to death or injury. The code forbids lawyers from warning others of potential fraud by a client.

Thus the question whether professional ethics is logically dependent upon normative ethics has been answered negatively in those cases where professional codes do not have a counterpart in normative ethics; moreover, in some cases they conflict with normative systems. In the latter case it would mean that to be socialized as a professional practitioner, one would have to lay aside, unlearn or renounce certain principles of normative ethics in exercising one's professional roles. But despite these differences, basic moral principles can be cited from which professional ethics derives some of its values. 'One ought to fulfill one's duties' is a moral principle, relating to the conception of responsibility discussed earlier in the chapter, upon which much of professional ethics rests. Without such a principle, whether explicit or tacitly assumed, professional mandates would lose their force because one could always ask why a particular act should be performed or another act should not be engaged in. But, it could be said that duty is a remote idea: for instance, why is it the teacher's duty not to use professional relationships with students for private advantage? This duty principle seems to be similar to the dictum, "Act morally." The issues lie in what it means to act morally and what are one's duties. It could be said that to act professionally, one must perform his or her duties; this means, then, that a primary duty is to act according to a professional code of ethics. Of course this still leaves open (assuming that these points are accepted) whether one should follow the

---

8. Lawyers pass ethics code geared to client secrecy. *Austin American Statesman*, 113:A5 (August 3, 1983).

NEA Code or some other code; and if the NEA Code is adopted in general, whether the rules are not subject to question and subsequent revision.

Consider a less general moral principle: "Be honest and trustworthy." Notice the NEA rule that says that the teacher shall not misrepresent his or her professional qualifications, or the rule which enjoins the teacher from knowingly making false statements concerning a candidate's qualification for a professional position. Why should these rules be obeyed? Not merely by an appeal to the authority of the Code itself but by an appeal to the moral principle, "Be honest and trustworthy," which the formulators of the Code may have also drawn upon in their deliberations (though one cannot be certain). In other words, the syllogism could be stated: One ought to be honest and trustworthy; making false claims about professional qualifications violates this principle; therefore, in complying with the principle, one should not make false claims. Thus what has been shown is that certain rules of professional ethics are logically dependent on normative ethics; other rules and principles are not dependent and are therefore independent. This means that adopting any given system of normative ethics is not a sufficient condition for deriving a code of professional ethics; however, it is a necessary condition at those points where professional codes are logically dependent upon normative ethics. Normative ethics could also serve as a motivating reason for complying with specifics of a code in such cases where the professional continues to question why he or she should abide by a particular rule and pushes it back to a principle of normative ethics. In other words, if a professional questions why he should not help out a friend (who desperately needs a position) by knowingly making false statements in a reference letter to the prospective employer, he could answer the question by recognizing that it violates the NEA Code, or by realizing it is unprofessional, or by observing a basic principle of normative ethics which he may already accept: Be honest and trustworthy. Thus professional ethics is at varying points logically and psychologically dependent upon normative ethics; in many other points it is independent and may override principles of normative ethics (as in matters of confidentiality with clients). The two areas are not interdependent or mutually dependent, as any dependence is unilateral, not bilateral.

FORMS OF JUSTIFICATION

One approach to justification is through the use of models. A satisfactory model exhibits an analogy with the phenomena to be explained in such a way that there is an identity of structure between aspects of the model and phenomena.[9] Thus there may be an analogy in certain respects between the model and the phenomena (positive analogy), whereas in other respects the model is unlike the phenomena (negative analogy). Atoms, for instance, are like and unlike billiard balls.

Models have been used in various academic disciplines: homeostasis, the brain as a computer, man as a machine, evolution, society as an organism, and others. Various earlier models can be found in education: the mind as a muscle (formal-discipline theory); the mind as a receptacle or storage bin for knowledge; Rousseau's unfoldment model; and Dewey's growth model, to name a few.

Thus professional ethical codes, it could be argued, are models of the kind of behavior that professionals are expected to observe in their practice. Thus the model guides practice and the professionalism of practice is evaluated with reference to the models. This is done at the more specific tangible points of the model — usually the rules — by observing what are one's duties, what one should avoid doing, and what one is permitted to do. Thus the rule in the NEA Code that the teacher should not knowingly make false or malicious statements about a colleague, clarifies one salient feature of collegial relationships, though it leaves open what should be the positive aspects of the relationship.

But though it may well be true that a code may be in varying degrees a model for professional behavior, it does not answer the question of justification: one can still ask why the code in general should be observed or why certain rules in the code should be observed. The code as a model does not answer this question but assumes that the model is worthwhile; its effectiveness as a model is a pragmatic one of how well the model serves to bring about the specified desired behavior.

Another approach to justification is to search codes for a supreme value or obligation. In codes for physicians, one can identify a central ethical obligation: a basic moral principle for resolving ethical dilemmas.[10] The Hippocratic Oath, which seems to be the foundation for modern non-Marxist physician ethics, is based on the physician's pledge to do what he thinks will benefit the patient. This principle is also found in the Declaration of Geneva and the World Medical Association's International Code of Medical Ethics; however, the emphasis in the American Medical Association's 1957 Principles of Medical Ethics is not on the

---

9. Hesse, Mary B.: The role of models in scientific theory. In Shapera, Dudley (Ed.): *Philosophical Problems in Natural Science.* New York, Macmillan, 1965, pp. 102–09.

10. Veatch, Robert M.: Codes of medical ethics: ethical analysis. In *Encyclopedia of Bioethics.* New York, Free Press, 1978, pp. 172–180.

individual patient but the obligation to render service to humanity.

Presumably if a central ethical obligation could be identified in every profession, then when ethical disputes arise they could be resolved by determining whether they support or negate the central ethical obligation. Even if this approach would resolve such problems, it may not be easy to identify such an obligation in the various professions—witness the status of the justice principle in jurisprudence. The earlier discussion about the clients of teachers and professors illustrate the problem. Is the teacher's central ethical obligation to the individual student, the class as a whole, or to school board policies? Learning procedures that may be best for slow learners may not be best for the class as a whole. The teacher's ideas about promotion may conflict with those of the school board. Is the professor's central ethical obligation to his or her discipline, to students, or to the employing institution? These conflicts are not readily resolvable in the abstract but must be examined on the basis of actual cases. Even if a central ethical obligation could be identified in education (which has not been done), it may resolve some conflicts but not others. For instance, if the promotion of each student's learning is said to be the central ethical obligation, it may resolve conflicts between duties to students and duties to professional organizations (the former would override the latter in case of conflict); yet it would not resolve the teacher's responsibility in handling two or more conflicting learning needs of students. Since teachers have limited time and resources, which of the student's needs should be fulfilled? The teacher could possibly appeal to a utilitarian principle based on the good of the class as a whole, or instead to a harm principle to determine what student would be harmed most by not having her needs fulfilled, or to a need hierarchy that holds that deficiency needs take precedence over growth needs. In any case, one has had to resort to other principles to supplement the central ethical obligation in order to resolve conflicting claims. Nevertheless, if a central ethical obligation could be agreed upon for every profession, it would offer some help in settling ethical disputes, though singling out such an obligation may oversimplify ethical responsibilities.

A third approach could be used to establish one or more central ethical principles. Academic freedom and its corollary—freedom of students to learn—could be used as examples. The justification can be developed by employing a transcendental argument. This type of argument shows that a statement is assumed to be true if some essential form of thought or discourse is to be possible. The Law of Contradiction (which states that p cannot be both true and false at the same time and the same respect) cannot be proved, since any proof involves it, but must be assumed by anyone who makes an assertion and by anyone who claims the law is false.

The AAUP Statement, as you may recall, views freedom of inquiry as a basic value. Standards are built into such inquiries by the various disciplines: the scientist, for instance, is expected to employ the scientific method, report findings accurately, open them to public verification, etc. To communicate with others in terms of organized inquiry presupposes that one wants to exchange ideas and knowledge with others; therefore it would be foolish to arbitrarily restrain others (including arbitrary faculty restraint of students). Deliberation would be pointless if we had no freedom to act on our deliberations; and one cannot consistently engage in such rational discourse with others and then deny them what is demanded for oneself. Thus freedom of inquiry assumes a community of inquirers, including students.

Those who would oppose freedom of inquiry, if their opposition is more than a flat, unsupported assertion, may try to show that such freedom is dangerous for students or society in general; therefore they would need to provide arguments and evidence to support their charges. Perhaps they might try to show that free inquiry for young students in sexual matters may lead to greater promiscuity and illegitimate births or will cause the political system to become unstable and precarious. But to uncover such findings presupposes a right to free inquiry, the dissemination of findings, and the right of others to examine and dispute the findings. Thus freedom of inquiry is presupposed in any attempt to persuade, to investigate, and to advance knowledge and understanding. Parenthetically, such freedoms assume a democratic society, for totalitarian states would usually restrict the right of inquiry, especially into political affairs, to high government officials and members of the established party.

A fourth approach is to seek an external justification for the professional code as a whole or its basic principles by determining whether a correspondence exists with a system of normative ethics. The reason for this approach is that if the system of normative ethics is widely accepted in the larger society, it is likely that the code too will be accepted by most citizens. In one sense this raises a political question that will be considered later in greater detail: Who should participate in making decisions about professional ethics? But even if it was decided that only professionals should be involved in such activities, it does not rule out a correspondence form of justification.

Though it might be claimed that professionals are best qualified by knowledge and experience to formulate standards of professional ethics, it could still be claimed that society is the ultimate beneficiary of professional ethics; thus if professionals want relative autonomy in this area, the consequences of their activities might be consistent either with a dominant normative ethics or supportive of a way of life (if in a democracy, supportive of democratic values; in a theocracy, supportive of prevailing religious values, etc.). And it has also been shown that professional ethics may in certain ways be logically dependent on normative ethics; in such cases, however, it is not a matter of correspondence but logical dependence.

This still raises some questions. What happens with such unique principles as academic freedom and confidentiality, and standards either prohibiting or regulating advertising professional services? These principles and standards do not have an exact correspondence in normative ethics and may conflict with some systems of normative ethics. One solution, which would still maintain an external source of justification, would be for society to permit such professional principles and standards so long as they promote a democratic way of life or certain values within that way of life (e.g., equality, freedom, justice, consent of the governed, etc.). Or it may be shown that certain citizens receive essential benefits from such provisions and that the administration of these features are not discriminating.

Or it may be observed that certain principles, such as confidentiality, are integral to the profession as a whole and to debar their use would seriously hamper the profession and reduce its overall effectiveness. Thus the promotion of these principles provides internal consistency, meaningful relationships, or coherence; moreover, the principles ultimately serve the public interest, despite their lack of correspondence with prevailing normative ethics, because without them the profession would be less effective in serving society. For instance, without special confidentiality provisions clients would be less likely to use professional services, relations with present clients would be undermined because of a lack of trust, essential information needed by the professional in handling the case would be withheld, and the like.

Yet there are times when a correspondence cannot be used without violating the entire basis for professional ethics (as in Nazi Germany). Here it is a moral, political, and prudential decision: moral in the sense of deciding what is the right thing to do in terms of one's professional principles; political as to whether one has the power to uphold the code in the face of hostile opposition; and prudential as to whether one should oppose the authorities or seek to emigrate and set up a professional practice elsewhere. Professions and their codes have an established history and sensitive professionals, as in the case of Nazi Germany, recognize the grave conflict between their principles and a regime that ruthlessly denies human rights and basic normative principles. Thus in such cases professional ethics may render professionals more sensitive to such injustices; yet these ethics may also make their practice untenable if they are loathe to compromise their principles.

So far justification has been explored internally in terms of professional ethics as a whole or from the perspective of an external justification, but as yet it has not been shown how the different aspects of a professional code can be justified. It is necessary to demonstrate that rules and standards are relevant to the situation in which they are used by showing that their scope and range apply to the situation; that there is no reason for not applying them in the particular situation; and, finally, that the rules and standards are not in conflict with other basic standards, or, if in conflict, that they take precedence. For instance, the AAUP Statement says that the professor should encourage the free pursuit of learning in his students. It also says that he should make a reasonable effort to foster honest academic conduct. If he assigns in class individual projects to students which will later be graded, to what extent should he permit students to collaborate? Of these two rules, are they both relevant in this case and, if so, how applied? Is the denial of collaboration also a denial of the free pursuit of learning, or is it a safeguard against academic dishonesty? Are there any other rules that take precedence over these two in this situation?

When conflicts among rules and standards arise, one can appeal to a central ethical principle or, as in education where a single central principle may lack a consensus, one could still appeal to basic principles. In fact, ostensibly a central principle in the AAUP Statement (in contrast to NEA and AASA Codes where a central principle is not evident) is freedom of inquiry. The full operational meaning of the principle would become clear as applied in cases where the principle was seen as being threatened or abridged or where conflicts arose over rules and standards.

But why adopt a given set of principles? Their adoption could be based on the notion that without observing the principles one cannot become a reputable professional person, as the principles substantially contribute to a model of what the professional person should be.

Another reason is that the principles contribute to or help fulfill the general objectives of ethical codes. Not all codes explicitly state general objectives; but where such statements are absent, objectives may be tacitly understood and can be drawn out by studying the document as a whole. When the general objectives are still nebulous after making such attempts, it may be more advantageous to construct a model of professional behavior that would stem from the code. Where the general objectives can be discerned or formulated, then an attempt can be made to see how the principles, both individually and in combination, contribute to the general objectives.

WHO SHOULD MAKE DECISIONS
ABOUT PROFESSIONAL ETHICS?

The content and thrust of professional ethics is shaped by those individuals and organized bodies that make decisions about its formulation, application, and enforcement. Since implementation and enforcement will be treated in chapter eight, our concern here is with issues of decision-making in formulation and application.

The nature and characteristics of professional ethics will likely be greatly influenced by the composition of the decision-making body. In other words, it is likely that if a committee comprised only of members of the profession make the decisions their viewpoint at best would likely differ considerably from a mixed group (laypersons and professionals) or a group of laypersons. Obviously professionals will want their interests represented, though they may also consider the public interest as well; laypersons would more likely consider public interests, including consumer interests, and how professional ethics can be made to comply with established norms and mores of the larger society. Final decisions made by mixed groups, however, may not diverge as greatly as initial differences in viewpoints because of the need to complete committee deliberations to meet deadlines and the likelihood of various compromises to achieve a working consensus.

Several possibilities suggest themselves as to who should engage in the formulation and application of professional ethics: (1) only members of the profession participate; (2) members of the profession and laypersons and/or public officials chosen by professionals; (3) professionals and nonprofessionals (the latter group not appointed by professionals); and (4) nonprofessionals only in initial deliberations, with eventual participation and ratification by professionals. Although a fifth alternative is logically possible, it is implausible but at least should be mentioned. Professional codes could be developed entirely by lay bodies without professional consultation and professionals would be required to comply with the codes with the threat of sanctions for noncompliance. It is highly unlikely that any profession would voluntarily accept such an arrangement because it would deny not only autonomy but an historical prerogative of a profession: the participation in developing ethical codes. Thus it is questionable whether a group could even be considered a profession if such an arrangement is enforced. Each of the other alternatives, however, are more compelling and will be discussed in turn.

It could be argued that only members of the profession should participate in the development of professional ethics because of the intricacies and esoteric nature of the profession that renders it incomprehensible or mysterious to the uninitiated. Moreover, not only laypersons lack understanding but lack requisite expertise that only professionals possess. Finally, the participation of unknowledgeable laypersons may seriously thwart the profession from conducting its business, which could be to public detriment.

It is true that there are many aspects of professional life that nonprofessionals are not cognizant of or, if familiar with, do not fully understand. Of course if it is actually desirable for nonprofessionals to participate (which has yet to be established), then either professionals could inform nonprofessionals about these practices or nonprofessionals could willingly take the word of professionals in such matters. It is also true that nonprofessionals lack expertise in drawing a will, performing surgery, and researching a doctoral dissertation. The question is: How important is this expertise in decisions of professional ethics? It may be of great importance in some areas and less so in other areas. In the issue of euthanasia, what medically can be done to keep a terminally ill patient alive without inflicting great suffering, and what are definitive medical signs of death (to know whether medical services should be continued) all involve considerable expertise. In contrast, to recognize that academic freedom should be supported may not require any special expertise (although it is true that the public at various times has not been supportive of academic freedom, this may stem from educators failing to fully inform the public on this matter). Even when special expertise is needed in deciding some issues, that in itself does not conclusively demonstrate that nonprofessionals should be refused participation—only that they will have to draw upon expert testimony in their deliberations (the testimony could come from outside experts).

Nevertheless, nonprofessional participation, it may be argued, would seriously threaten the public's interest because the profession would be unable to exercise its responsibilities and conduct its business. A case in point is that the Federal Trade Commission ordered in 1979 three medical societies (including the American Medical Association) to cease and desist from declaring unethical, interfering with, or advising against the advertisement of physicians' services.[11] The AMA said that they banned advertising to prevent consumer deception; whereas the FTC claims that physicians' advertising would be in the public interest. The point in raising this issue is not to determine which position is the correct one but to see that conflicts do arise when professionals do not have exclusive jurisdiction over ethical practices. But conflicts may be necessary if the public interest is to be fully served. Of course, as seen earlier, professional ethics also has special functions and benefits to professionals themselves. The public or its officials may grant the propriety of these benefits so long as they do not interfere with adequate professional services to the public.

A profession, as well as professional associations, is not a private club, fraternal order, or secret society. A private club may have its secret handshakes, lurid costumes, and bizarre initiation rites. A professional association, whatever services it performs for its members, has some relationship to a larger public. Some have suggested that a true profession has its ethical code and its

---

11. Veatch, Robert M.: *A Theory of Medical Ethics.* New York, Basic Books, 1981, p. 80.

authority to adjudicate ethical disputes accepted by the larger society.[12] One way for duties as a professional to be legitimated is to have the right to act as a member affirmed. Thus to the extent that nonprofessionals are affected when professionals assume their roles (in contrast to members of private clubs), then acceptance by other professionals may be insufficient. The principle operative here is that those significantly affected by decisions should have a voice in the decision, either directly or through elected representatives. The consequences for a profession which denies such participation may be to have the public refuse to recognize its professional status; denial of participation may, in the long run, result in calls for greater outside regulation of the profession (this assumes, however, that the public is acutely affected, sufficiently informed about their problems, and can organize for decisive action). One way to avert public participation would be to formulate codes consonant with normative ethical systems which enjoy a wide public consensus, although this may not avert minority disenchantment in a diverse pluralistic society (as seen in controversies over abortion and euthanasia).

A second approach in the formulation and application of professional ethics is for participation by both professionals and laypersons and/or public officials chosen by professionals to serve in this capacity. This approach has the advantages of ostensibly overcoming criticisms lodged against the previous approach, enables the public to have a voice, and makes it more likely that public opposition to such codes will be mitigated.

From the viewpoint of professionals, this approach is less desirable overall than the previous one because they must relinquish some autonomy. Of course if professionals have final veto over decisions of nonprofessionals, then there may be inconveniences of lengthier deliberations when nonprofessionals are involved but no real threat to the professional's interest. Even if professionals cannot exercise veto power they in effect could do so with this plan if they have the exclusive right to select nonprofessionals to serve and thereby choose only those nonprofessionals who are likely to support their interests. Of course not all predictions about a committee member's voting predilections will prove entirely accurate; but by careful screening, these problems could likely be reduced to a minimum. Thus, although many professionals and their organizations would likely prefer the first plan to this one, psychologically this plan would probably be more to their advantage by allaying fears of the larger public and thereby gaining more public support.

But from the viewpoint of nonprofessionals, this plan leaves something to be desired. Suspicions are raised that the nonprofessionals selected will be little more than a rubber stamp for professional self-interest. This need not

---

12. Ibid., p. 83.

be the case, but it is a distinct possibility. If nonprofessional interests, including consumer interests, are to be best served, nonprofessionals who participate need to be more independent of professionals; and though they need not be hostile to professional interests, they should attempt to represent the interests of the larger public. This independence cannot be assured when professionals control all appointments. Thus whereas the first plan is most favored by professionals and least by nonprofessionals, this plan is not wholeheartedly supported by either group.

The third plan utilizes professionals and nonprofessionals in deliberation over professional ethics with each group enjoying exclusive power in the selection of their representatives. Obviously this plan would appeal less to most professionals than the two previous ones and more to nonprofessionals than the other two. It has the advantage of bringing together two independent voices. One shortcoming, however, is that this plan may result in more stalemates than the other two unless rules are established to avert such problems or overcome them once the problems arise. Professionals could argue that nonprofessionals lack the expertise to be given a position of parity, and that professional autonomy is likely to be seriously eroded by using this plan. In contrast, nonprofessionals could assert that the services that professionals provide are so greatly in the public interest that adequate public representation should be present at all times. Nonprofessionals could cite the fact that professional organizations are not analogous to private clubs, and could adduce many cases where these organizations have created policies which ran counter to larger public interests or were harmful to certain segments of the population (such as policies that have had an adverse effect on the poor).

In the fourth approach, nonprofessionals would initially develop professional ethics with eventual concurrence and ratification of professionals. This would be an acceptable plan to some nonprofessionals because of their conviction that certain professional services have a great influence on the public, especially certain segments of the population, and on various social institutions; consequently, the public has a right to control the standards and practices that vitally affect them.

This plan would be unacceptable to most all professionals and professional organizations because it would deny what they clearly believe to be their prerogative and would seriously endanger their professional autonomy; it would also ignore their expertise in the early deliberations and likely lead to protracted conflicts when the plans were finally brought before professionals. Thus a code would not likely result unless nonprofessionals could exert veto power over professionals; yet if the veto was resorted to, professionals may only halfheartedly observe the code, attempt to sabotage it, or simply ignore it.

These contentions by professionals about the fourth plan, though they may be exaggerated in places, are largely sound and therefore this plan would be unwise. Of the four plans, the third one—professionals and nonprofessionals deliberate over professional ethics with each group enjoying exclusive power in the selection of their representatives—is the preferable approach for the reasons cited earlier and also because it is the most balanced of the four. It should be added that in using the third plan, professionals should have exclusive rights in internal matters that do not affect the public (e.g., dues structure, internal organization of professional associations, etc.) and that deliberations should commence with matters that clearly affect the public. Most professional organizations, however, seek to maintain the first plan which places professionals in exclusive control; but increasingly state and federal commissions, state and federal courts, and consumer groups are attacking certain provisions and, in some cases, forcing policy changes. The content of professional ethics will be affected by the type of plan adopted so that less selfserving provisions will likely be included in the third rather than the first plan.

In subsequent chapters, specific issues in professional ethics will be examined in greater detail. Chapter four explores teaching and the protection of student rights. Cases of academic freedom in the classroom, the ethical use of tests and testing, student dishonesty, the student's freedom to learn, and the student's right to privacy are pursued.

Chapter Four

TEACHING AND THE
PROTECTION OF STUDENT RIGHTS

Certain freedoms are needed in the educational process, otherwise teaching tends to degenerate into a propagation of official dogmas and ideologies. Professional responsibilities in the classroom and in related areas raise a number of important issues. Some of these issues are stated as rights to be protected and therefore one may have seldom considered them in relation to professional ethics; yet these issues do raise ethical questions that need to be explored and clarified. Issues discussed in this chapter include academic freedom, the ethical use of tests and testing, student dishonesty, and the student's freedom to learn (including the student's right to privacy). Though these concerns cannot be limited to the classroom—they spill over into the larger academic environment and, in the case of academic freedom, may encroach upon society at large—either their point of origination is the classroom or at least considerably influence this area of academic life. The success of the teaching-learning process is profoundly influenced by the satisfactory handling and resolution of these issues.

ACADEMIC FREEDOM

Academic freedom is the liberty needed to investigate, publish, and communicate knowledge in an academic community without administrative, political, ecclesiastical, and other forms of interference. Academic freedom, in contrast to civil liberties which apply to all citizens, pertains to the faculty of educational institutions. Academic freedom is needed in the search for truth, both in teaching and research, not only on "safe" topics but on those whose outcomes are likely to stir widespread controversy.

It would be a mistake to seek a definitive statement of academic freedom from which rules for every behavior can be appropriately derived, or a body of abstract principles from which a set of specific behaviors can be deduced. In higher education, the tenets of academic freedom have been developed and refined through a large number of cases.[1]

The concept of academic freedom may differ from one nation to another.

---

1. McMurrin, Sterling M.: Academic freedom in the schools. *Teachers College Record,* 65: 658–663, 1964.

In Great Britain the term usually refers to the freedom of the educational institution as a whole from outside influences, whether political or otherwise. In the United States, while this usage can also be found, it almost always refers to the freedom of the individual professor.[2] Academic freedom refers to five distinct privileges: classroom autonomy for the teacher, freedom of inquiry for the scholar, extramural freedom for the staff members, tenure protection for the qualified, and academic due process for the accused.[3] Of these privileges, this chapter will focus primarily on academic freedom in the classroom, but will also consider how extramural freedom is to be accounted for within the concept of academic freedom. Special ethical issues in research are presented in chapter five, while tenure practices are investigated in chapter six.

The Development of Academic Freedom

The concept of academic freedom has multiple roots in Western civilizations. A belief in the use of reason in the citizen's approach to life arose in ancient Athens, and educated Athenians enjoyed a fair degree of intellectual freedom. The rise of the medieval universities in the twelfth century ushered in the university as an autonomous corporate institution; the master or teacher was subject to powerful restraints and the inhibiting forces of traditions. With the Reformation arose a lengthy series of conflicts between Protestants and Catholics and hostilities among newly emerging nation-states narrowed the range of freedom in the universities. Loyalty oaths were required of faculties by Roman Catholic governments, censorship was rampant during the Spanish Inquisition, and organized religion controlled many of the universities of Europe.

Academic freedom began to emerge slowly with the founding of the university at Leiden in 1575. Some of the modern views of the use of reason developed during the Enlightenment in the eighteenth century. And at this time a secular, rather than religious, political state became the sponsoring authority for universities. Under this system of governance, universities were able to rid themselves of theological influences from which they had been controlled.

The modern conception of academic freedom arose in the nineteenth century German universities. The idea took root that the university is a place where scholars and students pursue truth, extend it through research,

---

2. Fellman, David: Academic freedom. In *Dictionary of the History of Ideas.* New York, Scribner's, 1973, p. 10.

3. Metzger, Walter P.: Essay II. In Gorovitz, Samuel (Ed.): *Freedom and Order in the University.* Cleveland, Western Reserve, 1967, p. 68.

and transmit it to others through teaching. German students were free to attend any university they chose and had control over the process of their own education. All the universities in Imperial Germany were run by the state; the student could wander around the country attending the lectures he wanted in preparation for nationally given degree examinations. The German student enjoyed *Lernfreiheit* (the freedom to learn). Though civil liberties were restricted for citizens and professors alike, the German professor, as master of his subject, had a guaranteed career as a civil servant and was free to publish what he wished and speak his mind on his subject—the right of *Lehrfreiheit* (freedom to teach).

With the founding of Harvard in 1636, a pattern of denominational colleges became the prevailing form up to the Civil War. Colleges were under ecclesiastical authority and there was little academic freedom, either in theory or practice. The sponsors of denominational colleges did not intend that there should be any significant degree of intellectual freedom, and faculty did not have much aspiration to enjoy such freedom.[4] While some glimmerings of academic freedom could be seen during this period, the main struggle arose with the rise of secular institutions—state and land-grant universities. During the late nineteenth century many of the leading American scholars studied in the German universities and returned to their country with the ideals of academic freedom and a conviction of the importance of research. (But as will be shown later, the freedom to teach (*Lehrfreiheit*) was initially emphasized to the neglect of the freedom to learn (*Lernfreiheit*).) Whereas the earlier denominational colleges played a conservative role in the culture, the newer universities built great graduate schools for research to enlarge knowledge and offer social criticism.

The dominant and controlling university president of the turn of the century has given way to faculty senates and the growth of faculty strength in establishing standards and reviewing cases of academic freedom and university governance. The AAUP first published its influential Conference Statement on Academic Freedom and Tenure in 1925; it was restated in 1940 and interpretive comments were added in 1970.[5] Encroachments upon academic freedom have occurred during Communist scares in World War I and following the War, the McCarthy period, and the excesses on many sides during the student protests of the 1960s.

Much less progress in recognizing and protecting academic freedom has

4. Hofstadter, Richard, and Metzger, Walter P.: *The Development of Academic Freedom in the United States.* New York, Columbia, 1955.

5. American Association of University Professors: Academic freedom and tenure: 1940 statement of principles and interpretive comments. In *Policy Documents and Reports.* Washington, D.C., The Association, 1973, pp. 1–4.

been made below the college level, however. Howard K. Beale, in a comprehensive study of freedom of teaching in American schools, observed that "Teachers in each century and locality have been allowed to discuss subjects that did not seem to matter and denied freedom on issues about which men did seriously care."[6] He concluded the research of his study in 1939 by doubting that teachers are more free today than in the past; in fact, he found more violations of freedom during the preceding ten years than in all the rest of history put together.[7] Matters did not improve much during the 1940s and 1950s. Then there was fear that teachers might be "subversive," and attempts were made to root out those considered disloyal. An atmosphere of fear and suspicion provoked anxiety and timidity in schools and colleges and tended to put a freeze on the discussion of controversial issues. The height of intimidation was reached during the McCarthy period of the early 1950s.

Even though McCarthy's political career precipitously declined after his colleagues in the Senate censured him in 1954, the fear of internal subversion could still be found. With the work of the House Committee on Un-American Activities and the intensity of the Cold War, the concern over security continued to be great. This concern was expressed in the employment requirements for government workers and teachers in the use of loyalty oaths. In fact, it was estimated in 1958 that out of the nation's total work force of sixty-five million, one person out of five had taken a test oath, completed a loyalty statement, or received a security clearance as a condition of employment.[8]

The loyalty oaths consists of two types: the positive pledge and the negative disclaimer. The positive pledge usually requires the prospective employee to swear or affirm that he will uphold the Constitution and laws of the United States and the state in which he seeks employment, that he will respect the flag, and give undivided allegiance to the government of the United States.

The disclaimer affidavit demands a negation of certain activities. The employee usually must swear that he has not been a member of the Communist party or any other subversive organization (as defined in the provisions). The disclaimer affidavit, according to its opponents, is the more serious of the two because it inquires into one's organizational membership and abridges freedom of association.

The New York legislature passed the Feinberg Law in 1949 and the Law

---

6. Beale, Howard K.: *A History of Freedom in American Schools.* New York, Scribner's, 1941, p. xiii.

7. Ibid., pp. 263–264.

8. Morris, Arval A.: Academic freedom and loyalty oaths. *Law and Contemporary Problems,* 28:497, Summer 1963.

was upheld in 1952 by the courts.[9] It authorized the Board of Regents to disqualify from appointment or retention, after notice and a hearing, anyone who belongs to any listed organization which advocates overthrow of the government.

The change in the Court's thinking from 1952 is dramatically revealed in a 1967 reversal of that decision.[10] The New York laws barring subversives from teaching in the public schools were held to be unconstitutionally vague and violative of the First Amendment. The Court held that the state cannot refuse employment due to advocacy of an abstract doctrine or passive membership in an organization considered subversive. Any loyalty oath which precludes employment without proof of a "specific intent to further the illegal aims of the organization" cannot be imposed. Such an oath is premised on the doctrine of "guilt by association."

Thus the disclaimer affidavit has generally not been upheld; but positive pledges, to which academics usually have less objection, have been found to be constitutional in several recent cases. Teachers can be required to swear that they will uphold the federal and state constitutions and "faithfully perform" their duties.[11] Teachers can also be required to swear to "oppose the overthrow" of the government by any "illegal or unconstitutional method."[12]

Thus loyalty oaths, especially the disclaimer affidavit, placed limits upon certain freedoms; these oaths affected academic life at all levels.[13] But in view of Beale's findings about the history of academic freedom in schools, loyalty oaths further restricted an already circumscribed situation. However, since Beale's study, the McCarthy period, and the height of loyalty oaths, academic freedom in both public and private schools has generally improved.

Through most of this century the Constitution did not protect teachers when they discussed controversial issues. The U.S. Supreme Court, however, ruled in 1969 that neither students nor teachers "shed their constitutional rights to freedom of speech or expression at the schoolhouse gate."[14] As with rights in general, this right is not an absolute one and can be limited when it conflicts with other rights. The Court would need to balance the teacher's rights and the state's interests, as employer, in the efficiency of

9. *Adler v Board of New York* 342 U.S. 485 (1952).

10. *Keyishian v Board of Regents of New York*, 385 U.S. 589 (1967).

11. *Ohlson v Phillips*, 304 F. Supp. 1152 (D. Col. 1969), aff'd, 397 U.S. 317 (1970).

12. *Cole v Richardson*, 405 U.S. 676 (1972).

13. For a discussion of loyalty oaths and other restrictions on academic freedom in higher education during the immediate post-World War II period, see: MacIver, Robert M.: *Academic Freedom in Our Time.* New York, Columbia, 1955.

14. *Tinker v Des Moines Independent School District*, 393 U.S. 503 (1969).

schools. Thus false and reckless statements by teachers that cause disruption are not protected by First Amendment guarantees. Nor is incompetent or irrelevant teaching protected. Most judges, however, have said that teachers cannot be fired for assigning controversial material or using obscene language in class; decisions must be made on a case-by-case basis that considers the teacher's purposes, the quality of the materials used, the students' age and maturity, and the effect of the material on the class.[15]

Why do elementary and secondary teachers have less academic freedom than professors? During the nineteenth century when the foundations of academic freedom were being laid in higher education, the question of academic freedom in the public schools was not raised. In a rapidly growing country in which the existing curricular patterns were the ones needed to achieve success, little thought was given to the teaching of controversial social issues.

Second, in order to gain support for public schools, it was necessary to eschew controversial issues. Moreover, it is doubtful that most teachers of the day, in view of their preparation, were able to handle them.[16]

Some held that academic freedom only applied to those scholars who are conducting research, not to teachers whose main task it was to transmit the heritage. This view excluded from the protection of academic freedom not only teachers below the college level but college professors who were not engaged in research. This attitude can still be seen in those states that make a distinction between the research universities and other colleges and universities in the state system as to policies regulating academic freedom.

A fourth reason is the more limited intellectual and emotional maturity of the students in which it is generally believed that older students need less protection than younger ones from controversial or dangerous doctrines. Moreover, secondary students, unlike college students, are under compulsory attendance laws and may have no choice in classes or teachers.

Parents generally have a closer relationship with public and nonpublic schools than with colleges and universities. Some feel free to visit schools and offer criticisms about the quality of teaching and curriculum content. Public participation may help to improve schools; in other cases where public concerns are misguided, restrictions of academic freedom may result.

A sixth reason is that college teaching is considered more professional than public or nonpublic school teaching. As noted in chapter one, professionalism carries with it greater autonomy and more freedom to exercise professional judgment. One indication, therefore, that the public school

---

15. Fischer, Louis, Schimmel, David, and Kelly, Cynthia: *Teachers and the Law.* New York, Longman, 1981, ch. 8.

16. Brubacher, John S.: *A History of the Problems of Education.* New York, McGraw-Hill, 1947, pp. 633–34.

teacher is gaining greater professional status would be the recognition by the public of a full degree of academic freedom.

Justifications of Academic Freedom

Academic freedom has been justified on both intrinsic and extrinsic grounds. As Aristotle remarked, "All men by nature desire to know." To be fully human, it is necessary to develop and use one's intellectual abilities. Whenever unnecessary and arbitrary restrictions are placed on inquiry, life becomes stunted and distorted. Thus, it is through free inquiry that individuals learn to sift truth from error.

The university, according to Russell Kirk, may not just exist for the sake of the community but for its own sake.[17] He cites Plato's Academy and the medieval university as examples. The university exists for the sake of "private wisdom and private needs." For twenty-three centuries Plato's Academy has been the model for freedom to pursue Truth. The Academy was not founded by the community but by private persons for their "private, professional delight." Just as the Academy's allegiance was to Truth rather than the community, the medieval universities were free because this was also their allegiance. Kirk's views notwithstanding, one could advocate the pursuit of truth for its own sake without accepting his historical argument, or could propose such other intrinsic reasons as the satisfaction of intellectual curiosity and the cultivation of creative potential.

Extrinsic justifications view academic freedom as contributing to democracy and social progress. Academic freedom fosters a genuine intellectual freedom for the entire community; and it is by means of academic freedom that the freedom of a people becomes articulate.[18] If democracy presupposes that citizens must be informed about the many conditions that affect the body politic so that they may intelligently elect representatives and participate wisely in social and political affairs, then an impartial body of knowledge is needed, free from doctrinaire beliefs and partisan politics. Thus academic freedom, along with freedom of speech, press, and assembly, is necessary if a democracy is to develop an intelligent and informed citizenry.

Many advancements in natural sciences and technology that have transformed the modern world emerged from university research. And many advancements in controversial areas of the social sciences, humanities, and fine arts would not have been possible without academic freedom to pursue

---

17. Kirk, Russell: *Academic Freedom: An Essay in Definition.* Chicago, Henry Regnery, 1955, pp. 10–18.

18. Dewey, John: Academic freedom. In *Cyclopedia of Education.* New York, Macmillan, 1919, vol. 2, pp. 700–705; and Riesman, David: *Constraint and Variety in American Education.* Lincoln, University of Nebraska Press, 1956.

ideas free from censorship and arbitrary restrictions. Thus the extrinsic justification for academic freedom lies in the benefits which accrue to the larger society.

Professional Responsibility and Academic Freedom

Yet certain rights and privileges carry certain responsibilities. It is not only that academic freedom, as previously observed, is not an absolute right; it is also a right that has been subject to abuse—not only by Congressional hearing committees, state legislatures, special interest groups, governing boards, administrators, and students; the abuse also stems from professors themselves.

Some of the correlative responsibilities can be observed in the AAUP's influential statement on academic freedom and tenure.[19] As for research, the teacher is not relieved of an adequate performance of his other academic duties; and if the research results in pecuniary gain, there must first be an understanding with the institutional authorities. While the professor is entitled to freedom in the classroom, he should avoid persistently introducing material that has no relation to his subject. The faculty member enjoys all the constitutional rights of other citizens; however, as a member of a learned profession, he should be accurate in his statements, exercise appropriate restraint, and indicate he is not a spokesman for his institution when he speaks as a private citizen.

These extramural responsibilities of professors have especially raised some misgivings and objections. The AAUP Statement ostensibly holds the professor to a higher community standard in the exercise of First Amendment rights than that of other citizens. The 1940 AAUP guidelines may be prudentially sound (insofar as she may be expected to exemplify scholarship, exhibit scholarly restraint, and not leave the misleading impression that her views represent the institution), but would their violation be unethical as well as imprudent? It would likely be unethical to deliberately pass off one's views in a public forum as not only one's own but those of the institution unless the professor has been officially appointed as an institutional spokesperson on certain matters. The important point here, according to a 1964 AAUP committee clarification of the 1940 Statement, is that whatever statements made by a professor cannot constitute grounds for dismissal unless they clearly demonstrate her unfitness for her position—and a determination cannot be made without a full ex-

---

19. AAUP: Academic freedom and tenure, pp. 1–4.

amination of the faculty member's record as a teacher and scholar.[20]

This problem seems to be related to a deeper philosophical issue about the justification of academic freedom: viz, should we adopt the general theory or the special theory? Briefly the general theory holds that academic freedom is an important subset of First Amendment civil liberty.[21] By espousing this theory, faculty members would enjoy the same rights as other citizens in the community and would not necessarily be expected to uphold a higher standard of public utterances. Moreover, academic freedom would not be looked upon by the public as privileges of an elite group but as a right that stems from the basic freedoms all citizens enjoy.

The special theory, in contrast, is derived from the nature of the university and how it can best achieve its objectives. This theory, according to John Searle, requires four elements: a claim about the value of knowledge; a definition of the university; part of a theory of knowledge; and a theory of academic competence.[22] The special theory rests it case upon the professor's competence in some discipline, the need for inquiry and the dissemination of findings. Despite the lack of general civil liberties in nineteenth century Germany, academic freedom could flourish in the universities by support of a special theory (not the one given above). A disadvantage to the special theory, however, is that administrators may feel justified in placing restrictions on the out of class behavior of faculty and students. Yet the general theory is hamstrung by the judiciary's failure to acknowledge a separately-identifiable First Amendment right to academic freedom. Thus, at present, faculty members can still claim their constitutional rights in the community while adopting a special theory or some other justification (such as those discussed earlier) for the protection of academic freedom.

Academic freedom is not designed to protect the incompetent. The teacher's ideas must not only be competent in the sense of demonstrating sound scholarship but should also be disinterested insofar as the classroom is not made a platform to promote the teacher's partisan political and economic views or proselyte for one's religion or pet causes. These purposes would subvert the purposes of academic freedom: to advance, extend, and transmit knowledge and understanding.

Faculty violations of academic freedom may lie more in the *manner* than the *matter* of expression. A violation of academic freedom may consist of

20. American Association of University Professors: Committee A statement on extramural utterances. In *AAUP Policy Documents and Reports.* Washington, D.C., The Association, 1973, p. 14.

21. For an advocate of this position, see: Van Alstyne, William: The specific theory of academic freedom and the general issue of civil liberty. In Pincoffs, Edmund L. (Ed): *The Concept of Academic Freedom.* Austin, University of Texas Press, 1972, ch. 5.

22. Searle, John R.: Two concepts of academic freedom. Ibid., ch. 6.

intemperateness of expression, intentional falsehood, incitement of misconduct. Intemperateness could consist of inflammatory name-calling of the
university administration while discussing university problems in class;
intentional falsehood could be instances where one seeks to win one's point
in class debate at all costs, or intentionally falsifying research data; and
incitement of misconduct could be the professor's inflammatory speech at a
campus rally that incites student outbreaks of violence, vandalism, or the
breaking of institutional regulations. The matter of expression is protected
even though the ideas presented are unpopular and controversial. Although
academic freedom does not allow proselytizing in favor of evolution, science
cannot be fairly and adequately taught by excluding it. Church-supported
institutions may want to teach creationism, but it would not appear that
science teachers must present information about creationism whenever evolution is discussed so long as the scientific community holds that creationism
is not based on scientific evidence.

The instructor should avoid the exclusive or one-sided presentation of his
personal views; differing viewpoints should be treated fairly and impartially
and the instructor's views, if introduced, should be clearly labeled as such
and only introduced if doing so will advance inquiry or if students sincerely
want to know about them (an insincere request may be for the purpose of
espousing the instructor's views on tests in order to improve grades). The
instructor should not teach something as final that is still being debated by
scholars. While the teacher-scholar is expected to pursue truth wherever the
evidence might lead, he cannot distort or falsify the results to fit a preconceived
pattern. The scholar's investigations are open to the careful scrutiny of
other qualified researchers.

The AAUP Statement on academic freedom and tenure holds that while
the teacher is entitled to freedom in the classroom—and this freedom includes the right to discuss controversial material—he should avoid persistently
introducing material that has no relation to his subject. Presumably (though
the AAUP does not say so) whether he could rightfully be reprimanded and
admonished would depend upon whether such actions interfered with his
effectiveness as a teacher, whether he posed as an authority in an area where
his knowledge was no greater than a layperson, or threatened students who
refused to accept his views.

Still, one might question the wisdom of the AAUP admonition. Although
a professor may not be an expert in another subject, she may have a
scholarly interest in it and have done some reading and study. As a scientist,
for instance, she may wish to point out the likely social consequences of
certain scientific developments, even though she is not an expert in any of
the social sciences. An economist, in discussing priorities in the federal
budget, may make the observation that manned spaceflights to the moon and

planets within our solar system are unnecessary in view of anticipated exorbitant expenditures and the present ability of scientists to gather much important data by using unmanned flights. The latter judgment, although lying outside her area of competence, is certainly justifiable in light of the topic of discussion. If challenged, however, she must fall back upon recognized scientific authorities for support.

But the courts have ruled that academic freedom does not protect a teacher's classroom comments, even though they do not cause substantial disruption, if they were completely irrelevant to the class and diverted class time from the required curriculum.[23] The ruling involved a St. Louis mathematics teacher who was dismissed after telling his class that army recruiters had no right to be at their high school and he urged students to push the recruiters and throw apples at them in order to get them off campus. This case, however, is different than the examples given above about the scientist and the economist because they made connections with the subject matter taught.

Thus, in summary, academic freedom entails professional responsibilities. Academic freedom in research does not relieve the teacher-researcher from an adequate performance of his other duties. Though faculty members should enjoy the same First Amendment rights as other citizens, they should make it clear when speaking as a private citizen that they are not officially representing their institution. The faculty member has an obligation to be temperate in expression, truthful, not incite student misconduct, not proselyte, try to present different points of view fairly, and not introduce material in class that is irrelevant to the subject being presented. Only in this way can Arthur Lovejoy's ideal be approached of the university as "the outpost of the intellectual life of a civilized society, the institution set up on the frontier of human knowledge to widen the dominion of man's mind."[24]

THE ETHICAL USES OF TESTS AND TESTING

Teachers are responsible for the continuous appraisal of student achievement and their own teaching effectiveness. To these ends various kinds of tests are employed. The purposes of testing and the use of measurement data are: (1) selection, clarification, and appraisal of educational and instructional objectives; (2) determination and reporting of achievement; and (3) planning,

---

23. *Birdwell u Hazlewood School District,* 491 F. 2d 490 (8th Cir. 1974).

24. Lovejoy, Arthur O.: Academic freedom. In *Encyclopedia of the Social Sciences.* New York, Macmillan, 1930, vol. 1, p. 384.

directing, and improving learning experiences.[25] Our focus is limited to classroom teachers at all levels and does not directly concern the specialized uses and applications of tests made by psychologists and admission officials. Nor is our focus on the relative merits of different types of tests.

In attempting to fulfill the purposes of testing and in working with students, certain ethical problems arise for teachers. Not all of these problems are clearly ethical ones but some may be problems of teacher competence. Incompetence is where the professional's overall work performance fails to meet minimum standards. In contrast, a simple test to determine unethical behavior is whether the act violates an applicable ethical principle.

Various rules and prescriptions about testing will now be presented and classified according to one of the three testing purposes stated above (although some rules may apply to more than one purpose, they are classified according to the purpose to which each rule most directly relates). The first purpose of testing is to select, clarify, and appraise educational and instructional objectives. To this end, the teacher will be expected to develop a system of evaluation for each of her courses. Even where testing is deemphasized and neither letter nor numerical grades are used, evaluation serves such various other purposes as providing students feedback and informing teachers about instructional effectiveness. Failure to develop a system of evaluation reflects more upon competence than ethics unless the system is required by institutional regulations and is deliberately neglected by the instructor.

Two other prescriptions can be offered to help fulfill the first purpose of testing, although they most closely bear upon the competency/incompetency issue than ethical/unethical behavior. Teachers should consult evaluation specialists when they encounter obdurate testing problems or suspect that their evaluation plan is inadequate to meet course objectives. Another recommendation is that as a result of test findings, the teacher will adapt and modify the syllabus to the needs and abilities of the class. The modifications may even include course objectives.

The second purpose of testing is to determine and report student achievement. The teacher should observe the principle of respect for students as persons. In relation to testing, this means that it is the teacher's responsibility to decide how best to administer tests to handicapped and foreign students so that the rest of the class will not have an unfair advantage and that test validity will not be compromised. Second, teachers must avoid handling tests in such a way that students could be pejoratively labelled (e.g., "moron,"

---

25. Payne, David A.: Measurement in education. In *Encyclopedia of Educational Research* (Fifth Edition). New York, Free Press, 1982, vol. 3, p. 1182.

etc.), humiliated, ridiculed, or in some other way made to feel worthless. As a corollary, invidious comparisons among students should be scrupulously avoided by the teacher and discouraged when done by students.

Another principle that the teacher observes is the pursuit and communication of truth. This means that the teacher needs to safeguard tests and testing procedures to avoid violating the integrity of the test and to discourage student dishonesty. Thus student dishonesty distorts the validity of tests and the subsequent reporting of student progress, it is unfair to honest students, and it violates the free and open pursuit of truth.

The teacher also observes the principle of respect for students' privacy. The teacher should ensure the privacy of students' grades and student materials submitted in class. This will avoid some of the outcomes mentioned earlier that should be guarded against: invidious comparisons, pejorative labels, ridicule, and the like. Moreover, when privacy is not observed, the teacher-student relation is compromised and the teacher's effectiveness as an advisor is greatly weakened. (Privacy, as well as student dishonesty, will be discussed at greater length later in the chapter.)

The teacher will comply with regulations regarding the administering of examinations and the submitting of grade reports. In accepting a position in the system, the teacher in effect agrees to comply with institutional policies, rules and regulations, even though by accepting the position does not mean that the teacher believes that each of these regulations is wise or sensible. Should the teacher believe that the rules governing examinations and grade reports are unsound, then he would have the right to make these known to the proper authorities and thereby seek to rectify them. But deliberately flouting regulations without calling their weaknesses to public attention, would be grounds for reprimand, if not more serious action. The instructor who pursues his grievances in these matters while abiding by the applicable regulations and who finally loses his case would not be entitled to disregard the rules thereafter as a form of protest because he believes the rules to be unsound or unwise—as the wont of institutions is to periodically enforce unsound or unwise rules. It would be necessary instead for the instructor to demonstrate that the rules either violate a higher set of institutional principles or some constitutionally-protected right.

The third purpose of testing is to plan, direct, and improve learning experiences. Tests are not to be used as punishment or to assert the teacher's authority over the class. Tests can be used as learning tools for students and to help the teacher see where instruction has been ineffectual. The instructor also needs to continuously evaluate his teaching and take constructive steps to improve it. The judicious use of test results is one way this can be done. Teachers are also expected to maintain regularly scheduled office hours for conferences with students about tests and other matters, and at many colleges and universities faculty are required to do so. Elementary and secondary teachers are expected to provide time to work individually with students and to make provisions, when needed, for private conferences. These prescriptions raise issues of competency rather than ethics, although it is the case that some teachers use tests as punishment and, in some cases, may humiliate students, which would raise ethical questions insofar as it violates respect for students as persons.

More directly related to ethical questions in the planning and directing of learning experiences would be the teacher's use of her position to indoctrinate or proselyte for her religious, political, racial, economic, or other beliefs, and using tests to reinforce these beliefs. This case would not only be an example of incompetence but unethical behavior because the teacher is denying students' educational opportunities and not respecting their humanity (by bypassing the use of reason and critical thinking). It may also violate her contract in a secular institution.

Thus, in fulfilling the three purposes of testing, questions about competence and ethics arise; even though more of the former than the latter. Ethical problems in the teacher's use of tests and testing pose serious problems, some of which are harmful to students; therefore teachers should carefully consider the full ramifications of the uses and misuses of tests.

Student Dishonesty

In the taking of tests and the performing of other class assignments, questions about student honesty arise. Such terms as "dishonesty," "cheating," "plagiarism" are used. What forms of student behavior would be instances of these terms? What are their causes? How can those problems be ameliorated? What ethical problems are raised for teachers?

By *cheating* is meant to deprive someone of something valuable by deceit or fraud, to violate rules—in this case institutional rules. Dishonest acts discussed here will be limited to classroom instances that include cheating on tests, examinations, assignments, illegally obtaining examinations, and plagiarism. Such other forms of dishonesty on campus (but not connected with courses) as lying to academic officials, stealing, and defrauding and/or swindling will not be discussed. Cheating is considered wrong because it violates institutional regulations, decreases the value of a diploma or a degree, it is unfair to honest students, creates an atmosphere of distrust, corrupts students' freedom to learn, and violates the free and open pursuit of truth.

How widespread is cheating? A survey of students conducted at University of Hartford and Boston University found that most students who took part in the survey had already established a pattern of cheating before entering college.[26] In India, where 340,000 candidates who annually take the higher secondary examination, nearly 17,000 students in the past three years have been apprehended using "unfair means" in six of the eight universities for which data are available.[27] The actual figures are much higher because most are not caught, some are let off because of a proctor's misplaced kindness, or for fear of student retribution.

What are the causes of cheating? In the Indian case, inadequate teaching in the 162 private colleges allegedly causes students to be ill-prepared for the examinations. Students at both Hartford (58 percent) and Boston (35 percent) reported that insufficient time to study was the main reason they cheated. A second reason was parental pressure. A third reason lies with faculty members themselves (this will be discussed under professional responsibility). Though not mentioned in the study, other reasons for cheating include academic pressures, large classes, short-answer tests, and lax administrators.

But explanations for cheating may also be found in ways the young develop a moral code. The conclusion of the Hartshorne and May studies of traditional programs of character education and religious instruction show that such programs have had little effect on moral conduct, as measured by experimental tests of "honesty" (cheating, lying, stealing) and "service" (giving up objects for others' welfare) and "self-control."[28] Rather than a character trait of honesty, the reason for cheating or not cheating tended to be situational: the tendency to cheat depended upon the effort required and the risk of detection; therefore, noncheaters were more cautious rather than more honest. Group approval and example influenced cheating and, consequently, classrooms in the same building varied considerably in the amount of cheating. Thus rather than divide pupils into honest and dishonest ones, the researchers found a distribution around a score of moderate cheating.

More recently, a developmental approach by Kohlberg has been applied to moral judgments and moral choices by delineating six stages of moral judgment.[29] Cheating does not decline in the elementary grades, according to this theory, because the child has yet to develop any internal moral values that oppose cheating. Instead, persons show tendencies not to cheat when they reach the fifth and sixth stages of moral development, and these levels

26. Walshe, John: Cheating prospers worldwide. *The Times Higher Education Supplement* (July 15, 1983):1

27. Abraham, A. S.: Exam cheat penalties stepped up. *The Times Higher Education Supplement* (July 15, 1983):6.

28. Hartshorne, H. and May, M. A.: *Studies in the Nature of Character*, 3 vols. New York, Macmillan, 1928–30.

29. Kohlberg, Lawrence: *The Philosophy of Moral Development.* New York, Harper & Row, 1981.

are not reached until adolescence at the earliest; many persons never attain these stages. Krebs found that only 11 percent of college students at the level of moral principles (fifth and sixth stages) cheated on an experimental test, whereas about one-half of conventional level students (third and fourth stages) did so.[30]

But if many students (as well as other people) never reach the level of moral principles, what can be done about dishonesty if we stick with this theory? Kohlberg has used some exercises based on moral dilemmas to advance students' moral judgments. For those students who after such exercises do not advance sufficiently, as well as those at the conventional level who have no opportunity to participate in such exercises, most likely they will need to be approached in terms of the way they relate thinking and acting.

At the Conventional level, Stage 3, is that which pleases or helps others and receives others' approval. One conforms to the stereotypical images of majority or "natural" behavior. Stage 4 is oriented toward fixed rules, authority, and the maintenance of social order. Correct behavior consists of fulfilling one's duty, respecting authority, and upholding the social order for its own sake. To reduce student dishonesty among students at Stage 3 the teacher could insist that cheating is "unnatural" or that most of one's peers do not do it; whereas the teacher could urge Stage 4 students to respect her authority, the authority of their parents (who also disapprove of dishonesty), and the threats that cheating poses to the school program itself.

Though Kohlberg's cognitive development theory is influential and widely known, not all teachers would likely accept it as fully adequate in explaining and coping with student dishonesty. A number of other moral education theories and programs are available, including values clarification[31] and character trait development.[32]

Professional ethics imposes an obligation on teachers to oppose cheating because it threatens the integrity of their courses as well as for reasons given earlier. The teacher's responsibility to treat students fairly and impartially, including protecting honest students, and their obligation to uphold institutional regulations means they must establish a plan to handle dishonesty prior to the first class meeting. The teacher could adopt Kohlberg's theory or another one to provide a logically-consistent approach to the problem.

---

30. Krebs, Richard: Relativism between moral judgment and ego strength in determining moral behavior. In Kohlberg, Lawrence and Turiel, Elliot (Eds.). *Recent Research in Moral Development.* New York, Holt, 1971.

31. Raths, Louis, et al. *Values and Teaching,* 2nd ed. Columbus, Ohio, Merrill, 1978.

32. Peters, R. S.: Moral development: A plea for pluralism. In his *Psychology and Ethical Development.* London, Allen & Unwin, 1974, pp. 303–335.

Additionally, some specific measures can be taken to discourage and control cheating among students who have not reached Kohlberg's principled level (Stages 5 and 6). Excessive academic pressures need to be reduced so that students do not feel that they must succeed at all costs. Grading on a bell curve also creates pressure and anxiety. Learning for its own sake and to satisfy intellectual curiosity should be promoted. Security of tests will need to be maintained, and examinations in large classes need to be adequately proctored. Teachers are notorious for using the same tests each semester; they will need to put more effort into evaluation by developing new test material each term. Large lecture courses will need either to be divided into several sections or to have sufficient proctors. When 5,400 students at 99 American colleges were asked about the prevalence of student dishonesty in the previous semester, half again as many in lecture courses reported instances of cheating on tests as in seminar or discussion courses.[33]

The study quoted earlier at the University of Hartford and Boston University indicates dereliction of duty among faculty: very few say they check out even a representative portion of sources, citations, and written materials submitted by students.[34] Many faculty members are unwilling to proctor examinations rigorously, acknowledging that they do not want to become "ogres in their students' eyes" as a result of confrontations. Another reason for the laxness is that professors do not want to get tied up testifying in hearing committees about student dishonesty.

To summarize, for teachers to fully understand student dishonesty, they may need to adopt a theory of moral education to explain what behavior can be expected, initiate measures to control and discourage dishonesty, observe their institution's regulations and procedures concerning such behavior, and assume their full professional responsibilities.

FREEDOM OF STUDENTS TO LEARN

Academic freedom, as originally formulated in nineteenth-century German universities, included the freedom of the scholar to teach and do research and the freedom of students to learn. Such provisions for students, however, were generally not recognized in the United States until recently.

The in loco parentis doctrine has been greatly stretched to include the determination by school officials not only of student conduct in academic life but in their social affairs and deportment as well. While university

33. Bowers, William J.: *Student Dishonesty and Its Control in College.* Cooperative Research Project No. 1672. New York, Bureau of Applied Social Research, Columbia University, 1964.

34. Cheating by students: Do teachers encourage it? *The Chronicle of Higher Education, 26*:18, (July 13, 1983).

students on a number of campuses protested university policies, the Vietnam war, racism, sexism, and other issues, restlessness also spread to the secondary level. As a result of dissatisfaction and litigation, some school systems have formulated more realistic codes of conduct which take into consideration the students' civil liberties.

Our focus is on those student rights in the classroom that are the responsibility of teachers, rather than rights on campus and outside of class largely under the jurisdiction and protection of administrative officials.

Some court cases involve freedom of speech. In Des Moines, several students wore black armbands to express their mourning for those on both sides who had died in the Vietnam war. The students were expelled because their actions were thought to be a disruptive influence. The Supreme Court held in the Tinker case that the suspension of the students was an abridgement of speech.[35] The act of wearing armbands is said to be "symbolic speech." The Court recognized that school officials have the right to control student conduct, but held that neither students nor teachers "shed their constitutional rights to freedom of speech or expression at the schoolhouse gate." The Court held that school officials cannot prohibit unpopular views because of their discomfort or unpleasantness but only those expressions that would "materially and substantially" interfere with the work of the school. The rights enunciated in the Tinker decision apply not just to the classroom but to all school activities.

Other courts have addressed the question of potential student disruption that might materially and substantially interfere with school activities. An expectation of disruption is insufficient to restrict student rights unless such an expectation is based on fact and school officials have already made an effort to restrain those who might cause disruption.

Students, in some secondary schools, have greater choices of teachers and more electives than in the past; yet these options are a matter of educational policy and not a legal right. Students have no constitutional right to determine teaching methods, texts, and courses.

In the Goss case from Columbus, Ohio, two plaintiffs from different junior high schools were each suspended for ten days without a hearing. Citing the Fourteenth Amendment that prohibits a state from depriving any person of life, liberty, or property without due process of law, the Supreme Court held that the State is constrained to recognize the student's claim to a public education as a property interest protected by the Due Process clause.[36] This Clause forbids arbitrary deprivations of liberty. The student needs to be protected from unfair or mistaken exclusion from school. Due process

---

35. *Tinker u Des Moines Independent School District,* 393 U.S. 503 (1969).

36. *Goss u Lopez,* 419 U.S. 565 (1975).

requires, for suspension of ten days or less, written or oral notice of the charges against him, and if he rejects them, an opportunity to present his case. Those students, however, who pose an ongoing threat to persons, property, or the disruption of the educational process may be immediately removed from school and given a hearing as soon as practicable. More elaborate hearings were not approved in the Goss case because they might overwhelm administrative facilities and resources nationwide.

In the Dixon case (which concerned college students but has also been applied to high school students) more elaborate procedures were approved for more serious cases.[37] These procedures are similar to a regular court hearing in which the names of witnesses to testify against the student and the substance of the testimony will be divulged, the right to cross-examine witnesses, to present witnesses in one's behalf, and the right of appeal are some of the provisions to be observed.

Not all student misconduct requires a hearing. As already noted, students who pose a serious disruptive threat may be first removed and then given a hearing. Everyday minor disciplinary matters also do not require a hearing.

The AAUP and other associations have developed a joint statement about student rights.[38] One part of the Statement concerns student records and protecting students' privacy. As to student academic records, they should contain information about academic status and not disciplinary cases. No records should be kept about a student's political activities or beliefs. The administrative staff and faculty members should respect confidential information about students. Protection against improper disclosure is an important professional obligation of professors in the use of information about students acquired in their roles as instructors and advisers.

The AAUP Statement assumes that faculty and administration have an obligation to protect these privacy rights, but justification for doing so is not stated. To supplement their statement some justifications can be offered. Among the justifications are the legal grounds based on the Bill of Rights (especially the First, Fourth, Fifth and Ninth Amendments),[39] psychological arguments grounded in a need to develop a selfconcept,[40] and on a moral obligation to respect persons.[41]

In 1974 Congress passed the Family Educational Rights and Privacy Act,

37. *Dixon u Alabama State Board of Education,* 294 F 2d. 150 (5th Cir. 1961).

38. American Association of University Professors: Joint statement on rights and freedoms of students. In AAUP *Policy Documents and Reports.* Washington, D.C., The Association, February, 1973, pp. 67–70.

39. Westin, Alan F.: *Privacy and Freedom.* New York, Atheneum, 1970, ch. 13.

40. Chapman, John W.: Personality and privacy. In Pennock, J. Roland and Chapman, John W. (Eds.): *Privacy.* New York, Atherton, 1971, ch. 13.

41. Benn, Stanley I.: Privacy, freedom, and respect for persons. ibid, Ch. 1.

which required school districts to develop a policy for parental inspection of student records. Confidentiality is protected by requiring parental permission before records can be shared with outsiders, and the Act establishes procedures by which parents can challenge questionable information in the records.

Returning to the AAUP Statement, it points out that the professor should encourage freedom of expression in the classroom. Of course this freedom does not exempt students from learning the content of the courses for which they are enrolled, but it does mean that students are free to take reasoned exception to views or data presented in a course and to reserve judgment about matters of opinion.

In conclusion, the professional responsibilities of teachers in terms of freedom of students to learn are to recognize their freedom of expression in the classroom and their freedom of speech in general, to protect their privacy, and to uphold their due process rights. The latter rights would mean not only cooperating with administrative officials to see that institutional interests are maintained but to testify on behalf of students when called upon to participate in any given case. Thus, academic freedom for faculty, in order to have a genuine learning environment filled with the excitement of ideas, actually requires as its complement the full protection of the student's freedom to learn.

Chapter Five

THE ETHICS OF RESEARCH

The conduct of research and the publication of findings raises many serious ethical problems. It always has. Strangely, these problems were not widely recognized until relatively recently, though the American research university began as early as the 1870s. Why this oversight? Or was it neglect? And what are these so-called serious ethical problems?

To answer these and related questions, this chapter explores guidelines on research with human subjects, dishonesty in conducting research or reporting research findings, conflicts of interest, secret research in the university, and faculty research with graduate students.

RESEARCH WITH HUMAN SUBJECTS

Concern over the rights and welfare of subjects in behavioral, social science, and biomedical research have grown appreciably since the 1960s. Dangers in the latter type of research were dramatically highlighted in the Nuremberg doctors' trials, which exposed the experimentation on prisoners by Nazi doctors and lead to the Nuremberg Code of ethical principles to regulate experimentation on human subjects. The Nuremberg defense took the position that the community takes precedence over the individual—but this position was rejected by the court.[1] The Nuremberg Code became the bases for the Declaration of Helsinki, adopted by the World Medical Association in 1964, and the "Ethical Guidelines for Clinical Investigation" adopted by the American Medical Association in 1966.

Public funding for research increased rapidly after World War II. The National Institutes of Health (N.I.H.) attempted in the late 1950s to adopt the Nuremberg Code for research, but the move failed because of problems in devising a single code for all of biomedical experimentation. However, with continuing government concern over these problems, the U.S. Public Health Service (PHS) in 1966 issued grant regulations mandating institutional review of grant applications as to the rights and welfare of the subjects

---

1. Redlich, F. C.: Medical ethics under National Socialism. In *Encyclopedia of Bioethics.* New York, Free Press, 1978, vol. 3, pp. 1015–1020; Freund, P. A.: Is the law ready for human experimentation? *American Psychologist,* 22:394–399, 1967.

involved, informed consent, risks and potential benefits. Provisions were applied to all HEW grants in 1971, and instructions for obtaining informed consent required full documentation. The Privacy Act of 1974 established provisions for record keeping, minimum standards for security and use of records, and provisions for individual's access to their own records.

Risks and Benefits

Research involving humans and animals to advance knowledge poses risks and promises benefits. Animal research and experimentation, though it has a long history and raises many ethical issues, is beyond the scope of our inquiry.[2]

The chief types of risks with human subjects can be divided into long-term and short-term harm. Long-term harm is either to the individual or society; and of individual harms, they may be either physical or psychological. Invasions of privacy may result in long-term or short-term harm depending upon the circumstances; in any case, it is a special problem that will be discussed later in a separate section.

Significant risks of physical damage to the individual may be found in biomedicine (psychosurgery, psychopharmacology, and psychophysiology). Though there are few recorded cases where subjects have suffered physical abuse, injury, or damage to their health, some examples have occurred. In a simulated study by P. G. Zimbardo where subjects role-played guards and prisoners, the researcher stopped the experiment prematurely after six days because of physical and psychological abuse at the hands of the "guards."[3]

Long-term psychological harm may be more common. Research studies may create anxiety, guilt, or loss of self-esteem. Some encounter groups, though frequently not formed for social research purposes, have increased anxiety or depression of participants for several weeks after the groups ended.[4] And experiments can create anxiety and identity crises. Experiments in which college students were wrongly led to believe that they had homosexual tendencies created long-term selfdoubts among subjects despite debriefing.[5] Humphrey's study of male homosexuality in public restrooms

---

2. See: Ryder, Richard Dudley: *Victims of Science: The Use of Animals in Research.* London, Davis-Poynter, 1975; and Regan, Thomas, and Singer, Peter, eds. *Animal Rights and Human Obligations.* Englewood Cliffs, N.J., Prentice-Hall, 1976.

3. Zimbardo, P. G., *et al.:* The mind is a formidable jailer: A Pirandellian prison. *New York Times Magazine, 122,* 38–60, April 8, 1973, sec. 6.

4. Lieberman, M. A.: Yalom, I. D.; and Miles, M. B.: *Encounter Groups: First Facts.* New York, Basic Books, 1973.

5. Kelman, Herbert C.: The human use of human subjects. *A Time to Speak: On Human Values and Social Research.* San Francisco, Jossey-Bass, 1968, ch. 8, pp. 202–225.

may have created anxiety over exposure and prosecution among the observed subjects when the research reached a local newspaper.[6]

Milgram's obedience research,[7] where subjects were instructed to administer to another person what the subjects believed to be electric shocks, has resulted in criticisms that subjects were entrapped into committing unworthy acts that changed their self-image and their ability to trust adult authorities.[8] However, Milgram arranged for a follow-up psychiatric interview with a selected sample of the original subjects a year after the experiment and the psychiatrist reported no evidence of lasting damage or traumatic reactions.[9]

Interpersonal relationships may also be harmed by some research studies. Participants in sex research, if disclosed, may find their morality questioned or become ostracized. Similar dangers of ostracism may result from serving in anthropological studies as an informer about community life.

Society at large may also be harmed by certain types of research and certain groups in society may be damaged. Minority groups and lower socioeconomic groups are more readily available as subjects for social science research because they lack power to challenge the research situation. Other research subjects who lack power are elementary school pupils, institutionalized children, hospital patients, and armed forces recruits. Researchers focus on disadvantaged groups to promote social deviance control, to help persons with social problems, and to have a more readily available source of subjects for study. The so-called Moynihan Report[10] was sharply criticized because of the image of black families conveyed and the danger the findings may pose for public policy affecting blacks. Black families were depicted as having high rates of illegitimacy, instability, a matriarchal structure, and harmful effects on children. The study may lead the reader to believe that these defects stem primarily from blacks themselves than from racism and discrimination.

The potential damage to society is that social and behavioral research may weaken certain social values. Polling, for instance, when it focuses on voters' intentions throughout the election, may distort the political process. Other research may erode public trust; and since a modicum of trust is needed to

---

6. Humphreys, Laud: *Tearoom Trade: Impersonal Sex in Public Places*, enl. ed. Chicago, Aldine, 1975.

7. Milgram, Stanley: Behavioral study of obedience. *Journal of Abnormal and Social Psychology*, 67:375, 1963.

8. Baumrind, Diana: Some thoughts on ethics of research: after reading Milgram's 'behavioral study of obedience.' *American Psychologist, 19*, 421–423, 1964.

9. Katz, Jay: *Experimentation with Human Beings.* New York, Russell Sage, 1972, p. 400.

10. Moynihan, Daniel P.: *The Negro Family: The Case for National Action.* Washington, D.C., Office of Planning and Research, United States Department of Labor, 1965.

have a society at all, this is a serious charge. Experiments have been run where a stooge falls in a moving subway and releases blood from an eyedropper in his mouth;[11] and psychologists have cried "shark!" on a well-populated beach to test public reaction.[12] These and similar experiments may weaken trust sufficiently that people will no longer respond to others in distress; as at the University of Washington, students observed one student shoot another but did nothing to help because they believed it was all part of an experiment.[13]

While disagreements occur over long-term damages, the short-term harm is more readily evident and less debatable. Subjects report discomfort, stress, embarrassment, imposition, and the use of subjects' time. Though these outcomes are not as serious as those in the previously cited experiments, the possible benefits from the research should warrant these short-term risks. Some of the harm can be minimized by appropriate debriefing procedures.

But in view of the dangers of the research studies previously cited, why should such research be undertaken? The reason lies in the anticipated benefits that may prove so substantial as to outweigh potential or actual harm. Benefits may take the form of advancements of scientific knowledge, the enlargement of public understanding, and the promotion of the general welfare. The individual may also benefit by making a contribution, enjoying the experience, receiving financial remuneration, receiving assistance with personal problems, or gaining improvements in one's neighborhood by special services provided the community or certain community groups.

It is difficult in the social sciences to claim objectively that a piece of research is of great significance, but it is easier to gain agreement on the value of completed rather than proposed research. The problem is further complicated because the social sciences lack systematic theory into which research findings can be integrated. Costbenefit analysis may provide some useful information but by itself is insufficient, not just that all benefits are not susceptible to quantification but that it is necessary to decide who bears the costs and who receives the benefits; since decisions about such matters cannot be derived from cost-benefit analysis, a theory of justice is needed. Thus the upshot is that when talking about benefits, one is primarily involved in a normative analysis and therefore more attention should be given to what this entails.

Decisions about benefits and harm could be made by employing one of

11. Piliavin, Jane A. and Piliavin, Irving M.: Effects of blood on reactions to a victim. *Journal of Personality and Social Psychology, 23*, 353–61, 1972.

12. Cited in Diener, Edward and Crandall, Rick: *Ethics in Social and Behavioral Research.* Chicago, University of Chicago Press, 1978, p. 72.

13. Ibid., p. 87.

two ethical theories: deontology and consequentialism. Deontology determines the rightness of acts apart from consequences. Duty and obligation are prior to value, such as promise-keeping. Thus certain considerations make an act obligatory apart from its consequences, certain features of the act itself; for example, acts commanded by God or the state, just acts, and promise-keeping. Kantian ethics and various religious ethics are deontologial.

In contrast, consequentialism holds that an act must be judged solely in terms of its consequences, either actual or expected. An act is right if it produces the greatest amount of good over evil as any available alternative, and is wrong if it does not do so. Utilitarianism is a leading example of consequentialism.

Both with deontology and consequentialism, decisions are made on the basis either of the act itself or on rules. Those who take the act approach would claim that decisions are particular ones that grow out of a situation, the facts and circumstances of each case. In contrast, the rule approach suggests that there are one or more rules that can be applied. The deontologist could appeal, say, to rules about truth-telling, promise-keeping, justice, or to Kant's categorical imperative. The consequentialist might ask not what action has the greatest utility, but what rule has; that is, choose the rule that will promote the greatest good for the greatest number of people (rule utilitarianism).

Now how would these two theories be applied to the questions about the possible benefits of a research project? One deontological principle may be that the subjects should always be fully informed about the most significant features of the research project and that failure to do so is morally wrong. A consequentialist principle would emphasize the possible benefits likely to accrue to the largest number of people; therefore, a consequentialist may approve a research project where a deontologist may refuse to do so. Take the case of prisoners who volunteer for medical experiments because it may enhance their record and thereby shorten their prison term. They are not fully informed of the health dangers of the experiment, but the possible benefits to society may be significant. Or let us suppose that they have been fully informed of the potential dangers but decide to volunteer anyway in hopes of shortening their prison term. A deontologist could still object to the experiment because she believes the experiment to be coercive by using compelling rewards. Thus she could enunciate the principle: No research project should in any way coerce subjects.

The deontologist may differ with the consequentialist in other ways. One prominent difference is that the deontologist may adopt a principle of justice that programs designed to assist persons of a certain class should be made available to all persons of that class. Additionally, those who are exposed to harm from some research should also stand to benefit from the research. In other words, the poor, minorities, deviants, prisoners and related groups may be disproportionately the subject of research but not the principal beneficiaries. The consequentialist may respond that their principle of utility, which says that we are to seek the greatest good for everyone or the greatest number, would satisfy the principle of justice because of the application of Bentham's dictum: "everybody to count for one, nobody for more than one." Thus the researcher is to count the effects of a rule on everyone and to weigh equal effects equally in computations. But if two acts distribute the same amount of goods in different ways, then the utility principle enjoins us to promote the greatest good for the greatest number. But the question can still be raised whether such a distribution is just, especially if certain minority groups, who have habitually been excluded, will be again excluded in the distribution of benefits. On the other hand, the consequentialist may question how much of the good of the larger society should be sacrificed to that of a minority.

The principle of nonmaleficence should be considered before approving research studies with human subjects. The principle holds that it is wrong to intentionally inflict harm on another person. Much depends here, however, on the definition of 'harm.' An individual could be said to be harmed when any of his interests are violated. Interests are those things the person has a stake in whether or not he is fully aware of them. A minor, for instance, may not be cognizant of his stake in the family's estate upon the premature death of her parents, but the courts will likely recognize the minor's interests.

But interests are of various types and significance; moreover, what may be a trivial interest for one person may be a significant one for another. A research project that consumes considerable time of its subjects would be a greater harm for someone with a cramped schedule than another with some leisure time. Despite these individual differences some generalizations can be made. Those research projects likely to result in serious physical or emotional harm would need to be prohibited. Even here, however, if full information is provided subjects about the nature of the project and its possible dangers and the project director obtains the subject's uncoerced consent, the harm is mitigated. The subjects would have to be capable of granting consent: that is, be an uncoerced decision by an adult in control of his mental abilities. Other serious harms are those practices that violate the subject's moral principles.

The researcher not only wants to observe the principle of nonmaleficence but the principle of beneficence as well. The latter principle says that one should do good or effect good. Thus if this principle is combined with nonmaleficence and both observed in practice only research projects which bring about good outcomes and no harm are to be undertaken. But this is an unrealistic standard to maintain because even under the most favorable circumstances some minor harms may result: discomfort, embarrassment, stress, imposition, and the use of the subject's time. Some of these minor harms may be eliminated or greatly reduced, but it is unlikely that all of them can be eliminated. This means that the beneficial effects—for the researchers, the subjects, and society—should outweigh the harm inflicted. One paramount value in research is to increase knowledge. But the expansion of knowledge cannot override the value of respect for persons, as was the case in the experiments of Nazi doctors. By respect for persons is meant, as expressed by Kant, to treat others as ends in themselves and not merely as means to the ends of others. Other ways respect for persons can be shown is to respect the subject's privacy and gain his uncoerced consent to participate (both topics will be discussed more fully below).

In conclusion, it should be evident that no simple formula is available to readily assess benefits and harms. But since projected advancements in knowledge should not override other significant values by sacrificing the individual or a group for the sake of the project, then it behooves authorities to refuse grants and the approval of research projects that may seriously threaten other values and principles previously discussed.

Informed Consent

Informed consent in human research is usually deemed necessary in order to protect the individual. Why informed consent? One reason is the principle of nonmaleficence that one should inflict no harm on another. Without informed consent the individual would be unaware of the probable risks and would be unable to weigh the risks against the likely benefits. In other instances the research may promise benefits to society or certain populations, such as those who are afflicted with a certain ailment or disease, but may have few or no benefits for the subject. Another principle is respect for persons, which can be stated not only in Kantian terms, where refusal of the researcher to seek informed consent would be treating the person as a means to the successful completion of the research project; it can also be stated that every person of sound mind, i.e., capable of deciding, has a right to decide what shall be done with his or her body. Refusal to secure informed consent does not recognize that right.

The first sentence in the Nuremberg Code states that "The voluntary consent of the human subject is absolutely essential."[14] Prior to Nuremberg professional organizations evidently did not mention informed consent,

---

14. United States, Defense Department. Nuremberg Code. U.S. v. Karl Brandt. *Trials of War Criminals before Nuremberg Military Tribunals under Control Law No. 10.* Washington, Government Printing Office, 1947, vol. 2, pp. 181–183.

whose importance has since been reinforced in certain landmark cases: Willowbrook, Tea Room Trade, Jewish Chronic Disease Hospital,[15] and Tuskegee Syphilis Study.[16] HEW was a leader in developing guidelines for informed consent.[17] These guidelines require a statement of the research's purposes; description of procedures; description of discomforts, risks, and benefits; an offer to answer any questions about the research; and instructions that the subject may change his mind at any time and withdraw without prejudice.

Informed consent, however, does not only protect subjects but serves important functions for researchers: it encourages greater care and self-scrutiny, provides valuable feedback from subjects, and likely reduces civil and criminal liability. The failure to obtain proper consent, if proven in court that damage was caused by the failure, would be treated as a case of negligence.

But what is informed consent in operational terms? When sufficient information about the research has been provided (its purposes, characteristics, risks and benefits, etc.) and the subject voluntarily chooses to participate, based on his own situation and interests after evaluating the given information, consent would likely be operationalized. The use of consent forms aids this process if the forms are handled aptly. The form needs to be accompanied by an oral explanation. If the possibility exists for a breach of confidentiality that may stigmatize the subject, then the requirement may be waived. It may also be waived where the research poses no more than a minimal risk of harm.

Some social science research raises obstacles in the use of consent forms: Telephone surveys using random samples cannot acquire signatures ahead of time; mail surveys, designed to preserve anonymity of respondents, would breach confidentiality; and anthropological surveys in preliterate cultures could not obtain informed consent. But in other forms of social, behavioral, and biological research involving human subjects, the securing of consent is appropriate and necessary.

Privacy and Confidentiality

An individual's privacy and the confidential use of information is threatened in some forms of social and biological research. Confidential information

---

15. Katz, Jay (Ed.): Experimentation with Human Beings: *The Authority of the Investigator, Subject, Professions, and State in Human Experimentation Process.* New York, Russell Sage Foundation, 1972.

16. United States, Tuskegee Syphilis Study Ad Hoc Advisory Panel. *Final Report.* Washington, Public Health Service, 1973.

17. *Code of Federal Regulations,* Title 45, Part 46.

relies on another's discretion in its use. Confidentiality is violated when personal information is divulged or made identifiable contrary to consent requirements. Sometimes this occurs when information is subpoenaed by congressional committees; in other cases researchers are careless or do not do what they claim in their research proposal.

Four important types of privacy can be delineated: informational privacy; privacy of personal physical access, contact, and intrusion; privacy from surveillance; and privacy of personal possessions. Let us look at each type in turn.

Some who opt for information privacy attempt to restrict the collection of personal data without consent, to have access to one's file and have the right to challenge and ultimately delete inaccurate and damaging remarks, to oppose the collaboration of agencies in free information exchange, and to prohibit the growth of centralized data banks.

Privacy of personal physical access, contact, and intrusion means freedom from interaction, touch, or interference. Examples would be the desire to be left alone, freedom from being summarily accosted, freedom from being pressured to socially interact against one's will, and freedom from offensive sounds. It would also include freedom from being touched, fondled, or to come into physical contact with another against one's will, and to maintain the overall privacy of one's body (which may include abortion rights). And it would comprise freedom from interference with one's actions except when such actions violate laws or infringe the rights of others.

Privacy from surveillance means freedom from unwanted observation, listening, and recording. In a public place most people do not want to be constantly watched by strangers or to be followed. Nor do most people want others to eavesdrop, to "bug" their home or office, to use electronic recording devices or take photographs or televised shots without consent.

Finally, through the Fourth Amendment people have the right "to be secure in their persons, houses, papers, and effects against unreasonable searches and seizures. . . . " Warrants can only be issued upon probable cause and supported by an oath or affirmation which would describe the place to be searched and the person or thing to be seized. Thus, in contrast to the three other types of privacy, this type is constitutionally protected.

These four types of privacy obviously are not equally important in research involving human subjects because some are more likely to be infringed than others. Privacy of personal possessions seems least likely to be threatened, while information privacy is the one most likely to be subject to violation; the other two forms of privacy would vary in the incidence and form of infringement, depending upon the type of research conducted and its implementation. Privacy of personal physical access, contact, and intrusion may be violated in different types of research, but would more likely be infringed in biological research. On the other hand, privacy from surveillance may be breached by social science research in naturalistic settings.

Privacy is thought to be good because it may be needed for persons to develop their full potentials. In many Western developed nations, however, the bias toward individualism and personal autonomy encourages the belief in the value of privacy. Yet even in cultures that are almost totally nonprivate, as the Mehinacu Indians of Brazil, they still have some provisions for seclusion; and even though a person's behavior in that culture quickly becomes public knowledge, some privacy can be gained even though the individual may find it difficult to do so.[18] Thus it may be thought that privacy is a universal human need that is more fully recognized in some Western cultures that emphasize individualism and autonomy.

In chapter four the grounds for justifying privacy were said to be various: by appealing to the Bill of Rights (especially the First, Fourth, Fifth and Ninth Amendments), psychological arguments based on a need to develop a self concept, and on a moral obligation to respect persons. Two other grounds not previously mentioned are the needs of autonomy and freedom. Autonomy is frequently connected to respect for persons and may be subsumed under that concept or it may be treated independently, as in the employment of autonomy in the right to control one's own body in abortion debates.

One way to connect privacy with freedom would be to attempt to establish freedom as a principle applicable to all persons in our society and to show how privacy is an integral and essential part of freedom. Here, as with other forms of justification, freedom is not absolute but must be weighed and balanced whenever it conflicts with such other principles as equality, justice, the need for knowledge, or another's freedom.

To be free enables one to choose the kind of privacy one desires, how and under what conditions it is to be exercised. The free person can develop a life plan and within that plan can construct a guide for one's public and private lives.

An abridgement of freedom may cause intrusions into privacy and constraints placed upon it. A lack of freedom may result in intrusions through failure to safeguard information, physical intrusions, surveillance, and lack of security in one's private possessions and effects. Notable figures may also feel constrained from appearing in certain public places because their privacy will not likely be respected. Thus potential intrusions upon one privacy may constrain action. Of course one can consent, for various personal reasons, to relinquish aspects of one's privacy. In that sense one's rights are not violated but one may be less free.

Privacy is embodied in freedom in the sense that freedom is a necessary

18. Roberts, J. M. and Gregor, T.: Privacy: a cultural view. Nomos 13:209, 1971.

condition for privacy; it is not a necessary and sufficient condition because one may also have to live under certain legal and political conditions to safeguard privacy rights. The exercise of privacy is actually a form of freedom.

The individual's right to privacy may conflict society's need for knowledge. Not all researchers are entirely convinced of the merits of the privacy issue, however. Brandt suggests that the concern with privacy may hide the fear that social science may undermine treasured ideas.[19] Brown contends that a balance must be sought between new knowledge and the invasion of privacy; he adds, however, that historically significant scientific advances have often been made by violating current ethical principles.[20] One might want to remonstrate against Brown that, unless the ethical principles could be shown to be unsound, obsolescent, or inapplicable, the research would be open to serious question.

The Supreme Court tends to uphold privacy against unreasonable government committees. Still, subpoenas by various congressional and legislative committees may not always respect the privacy of research subjects. But in a case involving the attempt by a private industry to subpoena the interview records of a researcher, a California court recognized that academic researchers have the same right to protect confidential sources as does a journalist, and to compel disclosure would stifle research into questions of public policy.[21]

Some procedures can be observed to protect privacy. Administrative and research records on individuals should be kept separate and not merged into data banks, old records should be automatically destroyed, common person identifiers should be recorded in all files while limiting confidential material to the original file. Research data obtained for one purpose should not be used for another without the subject's consent. Individuals should have access to records about them and have procedures for challenging misleading and inaccurate data. Many other procedures have been recommended, depending upon the types of research and their possible social application.[22]

DISHONESTY IN RESEARCH

Dishonesty applies to any breach of honesty or trust, whether lying, stealing, cheating, or defrauding. In the last chapter, dishonesty was discussed

19. Brandt, R. M.: *Studying Behavior in Natural Settings.* New York, Holt, 1972.

20. Brown, B.: The ethics of social science research. *Research Symposium: Social Science and Individual Rights.* Washington, D.C., American Society for Public Administration, 1968.

21. Culliton, B. J.: Confidentiality: court declares researcher can protect sources. *Science, 193*:465–67, 1976.

22. Boruch, R. F.: Maintaining confidentiality of data in educational research: a systemic analysis. *American Psychologist, 26*:413–30, 1971.

in connection with student behavior and the professional obligations teachers and administrators incur in regulating and discouraging it. Here dishonesty in research also raises problems of considerable gravity, but in this case the problems, if left unchecked, could undermine basic values in research and its beneficial effects.

One form of dishonesty in research is plagiarism, which is any uncredited use of another's ideas, information, or wording of material. It not only consists of lifting direct quotations from another source without documentation but paraphrasing another's ideas without giving credit. It may also take the form in a book of using the same or a similar organizational framework of another work, even though the content of the two works differs. With the neophyte lacking knowledge of the rules, plagiarism may be unintentional. One would therefore expect that the penalties would be less severe than in the more typical case of intentional plagiarism, except for the expectation that anyone involved in the activity should know and abide by the rules.

Is plagiarism an example of both cheating and deception? If the plagiarism is unintentional it cannot be a case of deception but it may be an example of cheating. Gert believes that cheating takes place "only in voluntary activities with built-in goals, for which there are well-established standards."[23] He believes that it involves a violation of a standard which it is expected that those participating in the activity would not violate. Cheating also involves deception because it gives the cheater certain benefits which, if known, would raise objections from others. But cheating does not always involve deception, as in the case of the boss who cheats only in playing golf with subordinates.[24]

Two problems with Gert's analysis are found in the notions of voluntariness and standards. One can enter into activities voluntarily but still do something inadvertently. But what he speaks of is "voluntary activities" rather than deliberate and intentional acts. Perhaps the built-in goals in his definition cover this feature in part. It is also not enough to say that the activities are governed by standards, as there are many different kinds of standards—standards in sewing a dress, composing a musical score, and conducting a formal meeting. But all of these standards are different than moral rules. The point is that cheating is a deliberate act, usually done to deceive, that violates moral rules or principles for the sake of gaining a special advantage or benefit. This means that deliberate plagiarism is an instance of cheating and a violation of moral rules but inadvertent plagiarism is not; the latter is a violation of standards against plagiarism. Only if we say that the person had a moral responsibility to learn the standards

---

23. Gert, Bernard: *The Moral Rules.* New York, Harper & Row, 1973, p. 107.

24. Ibid., p. 108.

governing plagiarism (and abide by them) could it be said that it is a case of violating standards and moral rules.

The cases of interest here are those of deliberate plagiarism by scholars and researchers. At Syracuse University a doctoral degree was revoked when it was discovered that the student had included in his dissertation 107 pages of a monograph written by someone else. The discovery was made by a professor who had written an opening statement for the original monograph.[25] Other universities also periodically detect cases of plagiarism in theses and dissertations. Obviously supervisory committees need to be more meticulous before granting their approval.

Other cases involve fraud by the falsification of research findings. A former professor at Mount Sinai School of Medicine at City University of New York fabricated data and published fraudulent results while a professor there in order to continue financing his work.[26] The fabricated data appeared in three abstracts, two published articles, a patent request that was granted, and an application to the National Institutes of Health (N.I.H.). At the University of Geneva authorities have notified the N.I.H. that it is investigating charges that one of its researchers forged data in a $70,000 project sponsored by the National Cancer Institute.[27] And a researcher, who had been a member of the faculties at Emory and Harvard, was detected with fabricated data.[28] The N.I.H. requested that Harvard repay $122,000 in research funds because the study conducted by the researcher was of no value to the agency, and debarred the researcher from receiving any future research support. At Emory, the dean of the medical school sent letters of reprimand to those faculty members who were responsible for supervising the researcher's work or were co-authors of his fraudulent publications.

The Association of American Universities, which represents 52 major American research universities, has urged more aggressive policies in preventing plagiarism, fraud, and other types of misconduct in research.[29] The Association insisted that scientists would have to ensure the integrity of subordinates' research, and be less tolerant of more subtle forms of plagiarism (e.g., inadequate referencing, submission of the same data to more than one publication by the same author). The report also urged that universities

25. Syracuse U. revokes Ph.D. in alleged plagiarism case. *The Chronicle of Higher Education*, 27:October 12, 1983, 3.

26. Former professor at Mount Sinai Medical School fabricated research data. *The Chronicle of Higher Education*, 26:January 5, 1983, 4.

27. Emory rebukes supervisors of researcher who faked data. *The Chronicle of Higher Education*, 26:June 8, 1983, 3.

28. Ibid.

29. U.S. universities tighten rules on plagiarism. *Times Higher Education Supplement*, May 6, 1983, 6.

take measures to protect the reputations of researchers unjustly accused of such acts.

Perhaps there are researchers who are more interested in gaining grants or padding their publication list than in searching for new knowledge, but at least they would appear to be in a minority. The few each year who are detected, however, may represent only a portion of the total number because few published scientific papers are closely scrutinized and because scientists, like other researchers, are reluctant to bring charges against colleagues. Peer review is designed to appraise the quality of proposals but not to detect fraud.

In science, if there were greater checking of research and replication of findings, more fraud could be detected. Co-authors should take more responsibility in carefully scrutinizing the entire project. Loss of colleagues' respect and penalties, such as those exacted by N.I.H. and Emory University in the above cases, should serve as deterrents. On the other hand, since research prospers best in an atmosphere of financial support, trust, and freedom of inquiry, it is vital that suspicion and distrust not be spread in order to protect the spirit of inquiry and investigation.

OTHER RESEARCH ISSUES

Secret research for the federal government has been an activity of universities since World War II but only became the object of protests during demonstrations against the Vietnam war. In the latter case students protested because of their belief that the Vietnam war was unjust and the university should not aid the government in prosecuting it. But the actual underlying issue in all secret research in the university, whatever the merits of the research projects themselves, is the conflict between open inquiry and the search for truth on the one hand and the commitment to be of service to one's country on the other. Since secret research violates the canons of open inquiry and the free dissemination of findings and thereby limits the advancement of knowledge (to which the university is committed), then secret research should have no place in a university. Each university should probably establish institutional rules prohibiting secret research.

The government can contract with approved research agencies not connected with the university to undertake secret research projects. A large question still arises about the faculty member's role in participating, whether part-time or on a leave-of-absence. So long as the faculty member does not conduct the secret research at the university, a prima facie case could be made that he or she should be free of institutional and collegial censure. Yet, by accepting a faculty position, does it commit the person at all times and whatever the circumstances to refrain from engaging in secret research because to do so violates the canons of free inquiry and the propagation of knowledge, canons one has tacitly committed to uphold? The questions are further complicated when it is recognized that most faculty members are not hired as full-time researchers but are expected to fulfill a multitude of teaching and service responsibilities; these latter responsibilities, except in the research universities, may even be given priority over research. Thus, to simplify our example, if we take the full-time researcher at a research university, irrespective of whether university rules exist at his institution regarding participation in secret research, his contracting to participate in secret research in an outside agency, either part-time or on a leave-of-absence, would appear to violate a tacit commitment to the values of free inquiry and the propagation of knowledge which helps give him a distinctive identity as a researcher. Only if the researcher could show that the value of the secret research project—a national emergency, for instance—overrides his commitments as a researcher could the researcher freely participate in the project and perhaps avert collegial censure.

This raises a question about the status of those full-time investigators employed in secret research who have never been employed by the university: Do the same commitments that apply to university researchers apply to them? Actually, these government or industry researchers, whatever one may think of the ultimate value of their research, by not accepting employment in the university have never made a commitment to these ideals and thus cannot be expected to comply with them.

Whether the research is secret or not, the university should not support research that is likely to be harmful to human life or impair human capacities. The university should also carefully screen research that involves animal experimentation. Whatever one may think about animals, their rights, and their relations to human beings, it at least has to be admitted from current biological knowledge that primates are conscious beings who can experience pain, suffering, and certain basic emotions. The ethical precept, 'Do not cause needless suffering,' should be observed. What types of animal experimentation are warranted is still a matter of debate.[30]

Research should not encroach upon teaching and service responsibilities. To this end the AAUP has stated that whenever an institution expects faculty members to engage in research, whether or not it leads to publication, then faculty workload should be reduced; and if only some but not all of the faculty members will be expected to fulfill this requirement, then this expectation should be made explicit and faculty work-

---

30. See: Regan, Thomas, and Singer, Peter (Eds.): *Animal Rights and Human Obligations, op. cit.*; Ryder, Richard Dudley: *Victims of Science: The Use of Animals in Research, op. cit.*; and Singer, Peter: *Animal Liberation.* New York, Random House, New York Review of Books, 1975.

loads adjusted equitably in accord with that expectation.[31]

Conflicts of interest have arisen as faculty members serve as consultants and researchers with government and private industry. The AAUP has provided a list of conflict of interest situations and university responsibilities in this area.[32] It may be instructive to see how one university has handled the problem. The faculty at Harvard University has established guidelines that require faculty members to report connections with corporate sponsors, including stockholders, before undertaking the research, and prohibits signing agreements that would limit the right to publish or discuss research unless it involved trade secrets.[33]

Another issue that has become controversial is the role of graduate students in research. Students complained to the California Psychological Association that they are being exploited in providing publications for academic psychologists. Faculty members feel increasingly pressured to publish in order to retain their jobs and consequently have made greater demands that their names appear on their graduate students' publications. Psychologists who responded to the graduate students' complaint say that publication credit should be given to all major contributors.

The issue is further complicated by the large research teams found in some disciplines, which makes it difficult to determine authorship; in addition, some scientific citation systems cite first authors only. Thus evaluating actual professional contribution to a research project becomes even more important.

The American Psychological Association (APA) adopted a policy statement to meet these complaints. Only second authorship is acceptable for dissertation supervisors, but even second authorship is improper if the supervisor only provides critiques, financial support, physical facilities, or editorial contributions. Second authorship, however, is obligatory where the supervisor designates primary variables, makes major interpretations, or furnishes the data base. In other instances second authorship is a courtesy: when the supervisor substantially contributes to writing the published report or is substantially involved in the design or measurement procedures. Disagreements, according to the APA, should be resolved by third parties employing these guidelines.[34]

Thus, in conclusion, the modest but promising beginnings of organized

31. American Association of University Professors: Statement on faculty workload. In AAUP *Policy Documents and Reports.* Washington, D.C., The Association, 1977, pp. 78–80.

32. On preventing conflicts of interest in government-sponsored research at universities. Ibid., pp. 81–82.

33. Harvard faculty approves conflict-of-interest rules. *The Chronicle of Higher Education, 26*:June 6, 1983, 2.

34. Professors' demands for credit as 'co-authors' of students' research projects may be rising. *The Chronicle of Higher Education, 27*: 7, 10, September 14, 1983.

research in late nineteenth century led to the emergence of the research university. The research university has had enormous growth since 1940 in research expenditures by the federal government and outside agencies — and with this growth has arisen a host of ethical issues. Though the researcher's attention is more frequently focused on the funding and the project itself, scrupulous attention to the ethical issues as well is integral to the growth and progress of worthwhile and humane research. Much progress has been made in the past two decades despite belated recognition of these vital ethical issues.

Chapter Six

FACULTY RELATIONS WITH COLLEAGUES
AND EDUCATION OFFICIALS

E thical questions regularly arise as educators relate in day-to-day activities with colleagues and education officials. These relations are not
static but are undergoing changes within and among educational institutions
themselves. Just as we saw in the last chapter that a host of new ethical issues
have emerged in research, new issues—as well as some older, persistent
ones—can be found in more mundane relationships.

Relations with colleagues and education officials are investigated in this
chapter in terms of ethical issues in recruitment; faculty advancement;
faculty dissent; and tenure, dismissal, retrenchment, and retirement policies.

RECRUITMENT

Recruitment refers to the process of finding and attracting new personnel.
It is an ongoing operation whose effectiveness is essential in maintaining the
vitality of educational institutions. Recruitment policies, however, differ
according to the education level and sometimes in terms of the type of
institution. At elementary and secondary levels, vacancies are determined
by the personnel department and unit administrators, with teachers usually
playing a negligible role. In contrast, in higher education each department's
faculty members generally have a role in recruitment and selection. This is
especially true in the larger, more widely recognized universities.

Dressel and Associates have identified at least three types of departments.[1]
The first type, the university-oriented department, is found in a moderate
size university with a strong undergraduate emphasis. Department members
focus on teaching and institutional priorities. Usually the dean's influence is
greatest in recruitment in this type of department. The department-oriented
department, found in larger, more complex institutions, exhibits emphases
of younger members toward research and older members to undergraduate
education and the institution. The discipline-oriented department, the third
type, has gained a national reputation for research and its doctoral graduates.

---

1. Dressel, Paul L., Johnson, F. Craig, and Marcus, Philip M.: *The Confidence Crisis.* San Francisco,
Jossey-Bass, 1970, pp. 216–218.

Its orientation is to the discipline rather than undergraduate education and the institution. Of the three types of departments, the third type is likely to enjoy the greatest autonomy in recruitment.

Let us turn now to the ethical issues involved. Rules that teachers should follow are based on one or more principles. For instance, the NEA Code of Ethics states negatively certain rules that pertain to application for positions and entry into teaching.[2] In fulfilling one's commitment to the profession, the Code says that one should not deliberately make false statements or fail to disclose facts related to competence and qualification. The rules also state that one should not engage in the following acts: misrepresent his or her professional qualifications, aid unqualified persons to enter the profession, make false statements about the qualifications of candidates, or assist a noneducator in the unauthorized practice of teaching. Some of these rules also apply to faculty advancement as well as recruitment.

On what principle or principles are the above rules based? The principle of honesty implies refusal to lie, steal, defraud, or deceive. An honest person is honorable in principles, intentions, and actions. It might be thought that a cluster of other character traits — integrity, probity, trustworthiness — might also be expected of the educator in these contexts, but to do so may be a case of supererogation. Professional ethics lays out minimum acceptable standards of behavior rather than impeccable behavior or the highest standards possible. *Integrity* implies such rectitude that one is incorruptible or incapable of being false to a trust. *Probity* stresses tried or proved honesty and integrity. And to be *trustworthy* means that others have earned complete confidence in one's integrity, veracity, discretion, or reliability. These traits may earn its possessor more rapid advancement but could not reasonably be required in recruitment except for positions of the greatest responsibility in the educational system. Those who possess these traits or are able to acquire them are more likely to advance, *mutatis mutandis*, to the higher positions. But which positions require these traits and to what extent is a manner for investigation.

Urmson holds that one should distinguish between what is morally obligatory and what is beyond the call of duty or supererogatory.[3] Although Urmson addresses morality in general rather than professional ethics, his thinking about supererogation may still be germane to our purposes. The minimum morality of obligation is society's moral code. One should demand only what persons can reasonably be expected to do; to demand more

2. Code of ethics of the education profession. In NEA *Handbook 1979-80.* Washington, D.C.: The Association, 1979, pp. 285–286.

3. Urmson, J. O.: Saints and heroes. In Melden, A. I. (Ed.): *Essays in Moral Philosophy.* Seattle, University of Washington Press, 1958, pp. 198–216.

would lead to frequent violations because of the greater demands and, consequently, the code would fall into disrespect. It would be supererogatory, for instance, for a physician to stay with his patients in a plague-ridden city or voluntarily join a medical team to go into that city to treat the infected. The consequence of Urmson's thesis is that it would be justifiable to choose the morally good rather than the morally better.

To insist that one must always pursue the better is to adopt the dictum that 'one must always strive to be all that one is capable of becoming.' Some may be unwilling or insufficiently disciplined to adopt or comply with this rigorous standard. In any case even if everyone complied with it, many persons may not be able to attain the morally better or the high standards of trustworthiness and integrity rather than mere honesty. Perhaps the solution lies in Hare's observation that "we use the acts of supremely virtuous men as examples, but only in so far as the traits of character which they exemplify fit into a coherent ideal which we find ourselves able to pursue."[4]

Various other problems arise in recruitment in addition to those previously mentioned. Though the matter of reference letters involves considerable individual judgment, it may be improper for an administrator to withhold information which may affect a teacher's competence. In a case before the NEA's Committee on Professional Ethics, a teacher was discharged by the board of education for behavior which was diagnosed as mental illness.[5] After treatment the teacher sought but was denied reinstatement and subsequently sought employment in another district. His former superintendent recommended the teacher without informing the second district about the teacher's previous difficulties. The mental illness reoccurred and the teacher once again had to be discharged; however, by not apprising the second district untoward incidents and unwanted publicity resulted. On the other hand, if the teacher's problem had been resolved and no longer affected teacher competence, it would be proper to withhold such information.[6] Administrators are expected to be fair in recommendations, to speak constructively, but to report honestly on matters that concern the students, the school system, and the profession. It is improper for an administrator to voice reservations about a teacher whose record has been outstanding merely because he wants to keep her in the school district.[7]

In the matter of contracts, a teacher may enter into oral negotiation with a school district and may still negotiate with other districts until a contract is

---

4. Hare, R. M.: *Freedom and Reason.* New York, Oxford, 1965, p. 155.

5. National Education Association: *Opinions of the Committee on Professional Ethics.* Washington, D.C., The Association, 1958, Opinion 11, pp. 26–28.

6. Ibid., Opinion 23, pp. 44–45.

7. Ibid., Opinion 25, pp. 47–48.

signed. Once under contract with one district, it is improper to negotiate with another district without consent of his present district to which he is obligated while his contract is in effect. Similarly, outside superintendents must be granted permission to negotiate by the school district to which the teacher is presently under contract.[8] Administrators are also enjoined from applying for positions indiscriminately and for those positions held by an administrator whose contract termination is not a matter of record; he shall also refuse to enter into any new contract until his present contract is completed.[9]

Anti-nepotism rules were formulated to eliminate favoritism shown on the basis of family relationships; and while these rules had a desired effect in some relations, in others it has restricted opportunities of qualified faculty members. The AAUP believes that such rules have unfairly limited opportunities and deprived institutions of qualified faculty members.[10] The AAUP does recognize that institutions should set restrictions on the individual serving as a judge or advocate with members of his or her immediate family. This means that faculty members should not initiate or participate in decisions involving direct benefits (appointment, promotion, tenure decisions, etc.) affecting immediate family members. But the Association does not believe in regulations proscribing immediate family members as colleagues.

With the advent of civil rights legislation in the 1960s and later Affirmative Action, discrimination has been greatly reduced in employment, though some minority group members and women believe that many improvements and changes still need to be made. The United States, with a long history of discrimination in employment, has generally made considerable progress in overcoming past inequities. Thus the legal machinery is largely in place to abolish discrimination based on race, sex, age, religion, nationality, marital status, and physical handicap. The enforcement of these legal provisions, however, needs to be improved.

FACULTY ADVANCEMENT

Faculty advancement, which includes salary raises, new and greater responsibilities, promotion in rank, and the granting of tenure, differs procedurally in public schools and higher education. Yearly increments in salary from public schools accrues from each year of satisfactory service and

---

8. Ibid., Opinions 15 and 17, pp. 32–33, 35–36.

9. American Association of School Administrators: AASA *Code of Ethics.* Washington, D.C., The Association, 1966, p. 25.

10. American Association of University Professors: Faculty appointment and family relationship. In AAUP *Policy Documents and Reports.* Washington, D.C., The Association, 1977, p. 28.

the successful completion of additional graduate work. In contrast, colleges and universities usually employ a merit system based on annual evaluated performance in teaching, research, and service, with research of greater weight in the leading research universities and teaching and service of primary importance in the smaller colleges and universities. Whereas in public schools principals, with occasional help from other supervisors, evaluate teachers, the locus of faculty evaluation is usually the department in colleges and universities, with senior faculty making judgments about junior faculty. But, as noted earlier, the degree of autonomy would vary by the type of department, so that in some colleges and smaller universities evaluation is found more at the college-wide level where the dean exercises considerable authority. Tenure decisions may be handled differently, at least in some universities, than decisions about salary increases and promotion. Since tenure decisions involve a long-term commitment to a faculty member, these applications may be sent from the department and the dean's office to an ad hoc administrative body usually appointed by the president and vested with the power to approve or veto candidates. As for the dean's role, according to Richman and Farmer, the dean who is not viewed as a scholar runs greater risks when vetoing promotion, tenure, and salary recommendations than one viewed as an able academic; however, whether the dean is viewed as a scholar or only a manager, it is wise for the dean to establish faculty committees for personnel and curriculum matters.[11]

Since the 1960s collective bargaining in public schools and higher education has grown rapidly. Efforts to bargain for the right of teachers to participate in policy formation has focused on promotion and evaluation, layoffs, and transfers. In 1979, there were more than 16,000 collectively negotiated agreements covering school employees, involving 49 percent of the school districts and 60 percent of the full-time employees.[12]

Rapid increases in faculty unionization in higher education occurred in the 1970s, with the AAUP, NEA, and AFT vying for representation on college campuses. College and university faculty were included in legislation in which public employees received collective bargaining rights in 25 states. Faculty were represented by unions in 1980 on almost 700 campuses; of these campuses, 60 percent were community colleges and 80 percent public institutions.[13]

11. Richman, Barry M. and Farmer, Richard N.: *Leadership, Goals, and Power in Higher Education.* San Francisco: Jossey-Bass, 1974, p. 254.

12. U.S. Bureau of Census, Census of Governments: *Labor Management Relations in State and Local Government: 1979.* Washington, D.C., U.S. Government Printing Office, 1980.

13. Martimer, Kenneth P. and Bragg, Stephen M.: Organization and administration of higher education. In *Encyclopedia of Educational Research* (Fifth Edition). New York, Free Press, 1982, vol. 3, p. 1377.

In public education, various proposals to weed out incompetent teachers and offer greater rewards for able teachers have characterized proposals of both politicians and educators during the early 1980s. These proposals include competency tests for teachers, merit raise systems, and master teacher plans. One problem of teacher evaluation is that of reaching a consensus on what is an effective teacher. The seriousness of this problem is frequently obscured by proponents of accountability who insist that teacher behaviors are readily susceptible to measurement.

Research on teacher effectiveness is one of the oldest areas of educational research, beginning in 1896. Early studies asked observers to list the characteristics of good teachers and various rating scales were devised. Attempts to validate these ratings failed: no correlation was found between supervisors ratings of teacher traits and measures of teacher effectiveness. By the 1960s researchers had turned to process-product research in which process criteria corresponded to teacher performance and product criteria to teacher effectiveness. This research differed from earlier research by defining the variables much more carefully and measuring them more objectively. Shortcomings, however, of process-product research show that it ignores pupil learning behaviors and teacher intentions. The problems, therefore, in research of teacher effectiveness have been recognized and progress has been made, yet the problems have not been solved. Policy makers, however, need to base their decisions on the most reliable knowledge available.[14]

The principle undergirding the rules governing faculty advancement is the principle of distributive justice. Our concern is with distributive justice (how scarce resources are to be fairly allocated) rather than retributive justice (how injuries should be redressed). In terms of particular acts, Aristotle said that justice consists in treating equals equally and unequals unequally but in proportion to the relevant differences.[15] This does not mean that people are to be treated alike: only that the burden of proof falls on those who would treat people differently to identify *relevant* differences. But here is the rub: What constitutes "relevant differences"? Rescher has identified many candidates for relevant differences: need, merit, effort, productivity, social utility, supply and demand, and others.[16] Of these relevant differences, merit is the operative criterion in faculty advancement. But what is meritorious differs according to observers, historical periods, and contexts. In the larger society, some have historically viewed wealth as meritorious; others have selected aristocratic excellence; and still others prefer athletic

14. Medley, Donald M.: Teacher effectiveness, *Ibid*, vol. 4, pp. 1894–1903.

15. Aristotle: *Nichomachean Ethics*. Translated by Martin Oswald. Indianapolis, Bobbs-Merrill, 1962, bk. 5.

16. Rescher, Nicholas: *Distributive Justice: A Constructive Critique of the Utilitarian Theory of Distribution*. New York, Bobbs-Merrill, 1966.

success. Prior to the Civil War, the American college was not involved in research and hence research counted for naught in faculty advancement; but since many colleges were church-affiliated, good character traits among faculty were expected and generally rewarded. Today, teaching, research, and service are the relevant differences on which advancement decisions are made, with the relative weight accorded each criterion dependent on the type of university, its mission, and the composition of the student body.

One argument against the meritocratic criteria is that rewards may be allocated solely on the basis of innate ability or inherited aptitudes; and since the individual had no hand in this matter, it would be unfair to thereby reward or blame the individual. Yet many cultures do reward the youth who inherits a strong and vigorous physical constitution that can be converted into athletic success. Musical prodigies and children with high I.Q.'s and scientific aptitude are also usually rewarded. Perhaps, then, merit should be based strictly upon acquired skills and abilities, such as skill in reading or learning to speak a foreign language. Yet to what extent is progress in acquiring these skills based on genetic differences? Whatever the skill, if the above plan is followed, genetic and acquired differences would have to be separated (which with most skills would be difficult to do). But there may be some skills or abilities that derive solely from practice, perseverance, and drill; these skills or abilities would be the object of merit. However, now the relevant differences have shifted from merit to effort. Perhaps effort should be rewarded or rewarded more than it currently is rewarded, but it would not be the primary consideration in faculty advancement because effort alone, without native talent and a nurturing environment, is no assurance of acquiring a requisite level of competency, even though without a minimum level of effort few would likely succeed. Thus with effort as the sole or even primary criterion, the university may advance incompetent or mediocre faculty members to the highest rank and into key teaching and decision-making positions.

But that leaves us with the recognition that merit programs for faculty and administrators may actually be rewarding a combination of native abilities, capitalizing on a nurturing environment, and effort. The nurturing environment or the lack thereof, especially in childhood, is something the individual has little or no control over; whereas in adulthood one can attempt to arrange an environment that will help to promote desired abilities. Thus merit is awarded by using one criterion not under the individual's control and a second not under individual control until the important formative period has passed. Consequently, one is partly rewarded for a favorable genetic endowment and being reared by a family that makes wise use of educational resources. Since the provision of such an environment is partly a function of family income, the poor are usually disadvantaged by the use of merit criteria. The poor and minorities, however, have been aided by recruitment goals designed to interview and seek out more qualified applicants from these groups.

Thus meritocratic criteria reward native ability, a nurturing environment, and individual effort. Though not formally recognized, it also rewards those individuals who have good interpersonal relations and are skilled in university politics. Thus the merit process, especially tenure decisions, considers these informal, less tangible factors in long-term appointments in addition to formal merit criteria.

What grounds can be adduced for accepting a principle of justice? Obviously this is not a question for a judge because it already regulates his or her professional functions. But it is less evident why others should adopt such a principle. Rawls has argued that we are committed to adopt the principle because we are engaged with others in joint activities designed to promote common and complimentary interests; thus we cannot expect others to respect our interests if we do not respect theirs.[17] Peters takes a different approach to justification.[18] He finds justice a limiting principle that stipulates the desirability of making categories on relevant grounds and the undesirability of exceptions on irrelevant grounds. The principle, he claims, is presupposed in attempts to justify conduct or answer the question of "What ought I to do?" Any answer to the question could not be accepted or rejected unless there were grounds of relevance for doing so. Moral discourse would make no sense without rules for relevance, and justice is built into the concept of a general rule. Those who tell others that there is no need to justify conduct are using practical discourse to do so; and since rules of relevance are built into practical discourse, such persons are presupposing the principle of justice while seeking to ban it or avoid it.

Once justification for using the principle is satisfied, one could turn to making decisions about what will count as relevant reasons for distinctions. Rawls attempts to derive ultimate principles of justice to regulate an ideal "well-ordered society."[19] His method of doing so falls within the tradition of social contract theory. A group of hypothetical persons are imagined to have gathered together voluntarily for the purpose of designing institutions to regulate their future lives. In this "original position" persons operate from a "veil of ignorance": they lack knowledge of facts about themselves and others, though they have much knowledge about other things—science, economics, the effects of social isolation. Thus they have broad general knowledge but particular ignorance. This means that they have to choose

17. Rawls, John: Justice is fairness. *Philosophical Review,* 67, 164–94, 1958.

18. Peters, R. S.: *Ethics and Education.* Atlanta, Scott, Foresman, 1967, pp. 49–54.

19. Rawls, John: *A Theory of Justice.* Cambridge, Harvard University Press, 1971.

their principles disinterestedly: they cannot be lobbyist for any particular personal, familial, or class interests.

Although it is obviously not possible for educators to make choices about justice in this manner because they are not in Rawls' original position and, consequently, cannot be entirely disinterested. But they can adopt principles that, when applied, do not cause avoidable harm to others or give some group an unfair advantage or aggrandize power to a group so that the group effectively excludes others from benefits, even though the dominant group may claim their acquisition and use of power is "democratic." This does not mean that no distinctions are to be made. Parents are expected to have more decision-making power than children, owners of firms than workers, and tenured more than nontenured faculty. Thus relations can be superordinate-subordinate and still be just if fair and relevant principles are followed.

One way to avoid acting unjustly is to know what are the principle injustices. **Invidious discrimination,** one ground of injustice, would involve arbitrary unequal treatment in developing and enforcing rules or in distributing burdens and benefits. Thus rules that arbitrarily exclude people from benefits or unequally treat people on grounds of race, sex, ethnicity, or religion would be guilty of invidious discrimination. Affirmative Action and other civil rights legislation have considerably reduced but not entirely overcome invidious discrimination. The difficulties that women earlier encountered in gaining tenure in some departments, the unwritten prohibitions by some universities in employing Jews, and segregated faculties that historically brought about all-black colleges and all-white colleges are cases in point.

Judgmental injustice is a second type of injustice. It consists in making unfair judgments of other persons—as individuals, and their activities and achievements. The AASA warns the school administrator that his or her judgment should not be clouded by any member of the school staff because of their rank, popularity, social standing, or position so as to conceal or condone unethical conduct. Nor should the administrator permit strong and unscrupulous persons to seize power and responsibility which is not their own.[20]

An earlier version of the NEA Code of Ethics enjoined teachers to "Speak constructively of other teachers, but report honestly to responsible persons in matters involving the welfare of students, the school system, and the profession."[21] The current NEA Code of Ethics obliges teachers not to intentionally expose students to embarrassment or disparagement, and urges

---

20. American Association of School Administrators: *The AASA Code of Ethics*, p. 29.

21. National Education Association: *Opinions of the Committee on Professional Ethics*, p. 75.

teachers not to knowingly make false or malicious statements about a colleague.[22]

Exploitation is a third type of injustice. It involves making improper use of another for one's own advantage by violating another's trust, manipulation of another's natural handicaps, or deliberately disadvantaging them in some competitive or joint undertaking. One of the most prominent forms of exploitation is sexual harassment.

Sexual harassment, according to the Equal Opportunity Commission, is "unwelcome sexual advances, requests for sexual favors and other verbal or physical conduct of a sexual nature." Such actions become illegal whenever a woman's reaction to such conduct is made a basis for employment decisions or substantially interferes with work performance or creates an intimidating or offensive work environment. Sexual harassment is a violation of many state laws as well as Title VII of the Civil Rights Act.

In a survey at Harvard University of all arts and sciences faculty, graduate and undergraduate students, both male and female, 34 percent of female undergraduates (and a smattering of men), 41 percent of female graduate students, and 49 percent of nontenure women faculty reported experiencing some sexual harassment, ranging from verbal abuse to assault.[23] Men in the survey tended to define harassment as sexual relations or assault, but only 2 percent of untenured women and 1 percent of graduate students experienced sexual abuse. Women, in contrast, included within their definition of sexual harassment demeaning remarks and behavior that make them uncomfortable. This situation is not limited to Harvard: a study at the University of Florida in the 1981–82 academic year reported that 31 percent of women graduate students and 26 percent of undergraduate women had professors to make unwanted advances. And the American Association of American Colleges estimates that 20 percent of all female students — 125,000 each year — experience sexual harassment.[24]

In addition to pertinent legislation and various types of campus grievance procedures that either are operational or have been advocated to ameliorate the problem, the University of Michigan affirmative action task force developed a video-tape that dramatizes a dozen examples of sexual harassment. Students are also given any of six university numbers to call for help with their problems. This combination of approaches is currently being tried on 40 other campuses.[25]

---

22. National Education Association: Code of ethics of the education profession, *op. cit.*, Principle I:5 and Principle II:7.

23. Fair Harvard, are you fair? *Time, 122,* 109, November 14, 1983.

24. Colleges to teach coeds to react to harassment: *Austin American Statesman, 113,* E1, November 16, 1983.

25. Ibid.

Returning once again to the criteria for faculty advancement, it is important that stated criteria actually be employed in faculty advancement rather than as "window-dressing" or a deception that cloaks a hidden agenda. Lewis reviewed numerous studies of publication productivity in various disciplines and concluded the "publish or perish" dogma is largely a fraud. Although to publish nothing at a major university will bring downward mobility, those who publish frequently in reputable journals will receive some rewards—these rewards, however, could be marginal. For 80 or 90 percent of academics, except for those in a dozen or so prestige institutions, the publish or perish threat is empty. About 90 percent of all major publications come from the top 25 doctorate-granting institutions.

The use of the publish or perish dogma, Lewis concludes, derives from a number of reasons: to conceal complicated institutional decisions about the true reasons faculty were terminated; maintain control over persons by the fear of losing their positions; help maintain the status quo by diverting attention from department affairs; and convey to faculty that objective standards of evaluation are being used when actually decisions are subjective.[26]

Whether one agrees with Lewis' explanation for widespread belief in the publish or perish dogma, the evidence that he cites from his study and related ones is substantial that publish or perish is really a myth for most academics. Thus fairness in evaluation would include the adoption of evaluative criteria that will actually be used in practice. If publication is not genuinely valued or has relatively low priority, then this information should be known by faculty members so that they can pursue other activities that will lead to more rapid advancement, should they so choose. In fact, if the publish or perish doctrine were actually in effect, a much higher percentage of faculty would be terminated because sufficient journal space and other outlets are not presently available to accommodate more than a small fraction of the anticipated deluge of manuscripts—and would not likely be available in the immediate future because of costs of starting many new journals, editors' desire for journal selectivity, and the geometric leap in the number of publications that would lead to further protests from scholars of the impossibility of staying abreast of one's field.

FACULTY DISSENT

Faculty dissent to institutional policies and practices in higher education finds outlets in the departments, the faculty senate, before administrators, occasionally before the board of trustees, and in grievance committees. Institutional rules may state that faculty members are granted freedom in teaching and research with the understanding they will still be expected to fulfill their role responsibilities for meeting classes, holding regular office hours for academic counseling and advising, serving on faculty committees, performing assigned administrative tasks, and the like.

One might presume that if professors enjoy a large role in governance that the need for dissent that violates institutional rules would be considerably abated. Just as we have seen earlier that the forms of departmental participation depend upon the type of department and its mission, the professor's participation in governance may vary according to the institution and the opportunities afforded. According to a study by Baldridge and Others, most faculty are more interested in teaching and research than administration and would prefer to leave administrative responsibilities to administrators.[27] The dominant pattern is a lack of faculty participation. Only a handful of faculty get deeply involved—such as department chairpersons, senior professors, and "faculty politicians." Increase in rank generally brings a requirement of greater institutional participation. Some variation in participation may be found by specialty: social scientists and humanists, Baldridge reports, have the highest participation. In any case, a small "power elite" and a mass of inactive people can be observed. But about one-fourth of the faculty engage in activities outside of the regular channels, and 28 percent of the faculty report that they "sometimes" or "regularly" work with unions to shape policy. Although most campuses in the Baldridge study had academic senates, on most campuses these bodies were found to be weak and ineffective. Senates do not deal effectively with substantive matters at most institutions; these issues are handled instead at the department level and by administrators.[28]

The point in this review is that there are a number of institutional mechanisms of varying degrees of effectiveness to ventilate faculty grievances. And with the growth of unions in higher education, faculty members have bargaining agents to represent their views and are therefore more likely to view themselves in an adversarial relationship with administrators.

With about 86 percent of public school teachers today members of either the National Education Association (NEA) or the American Federation of Teachers (AFT), dissent is likely to be expressed through union representatives, even though some teachers may decide to protest singly or in groups against certain policies. In Detroit Public Schools, the teacher can seek to resolve disputes with his or her immediate supervisor and, if not resolved by informal means, a formal complaint may be filed with the principal, who would be obligated to discuss it with the complainant and a union

27. Baldridge, J. Victor, et al.: *Policy Making and Effective Leadership*. San Francisco, Jossey-Bass, 1978, p. 75.

28. Ibid., pp. 74–82.

representative; the principal would be expected to issue a written decision in ten days or less. If the complainant remains dissatisfied with the principal's decision, further adjudication may be offered in some school districts in which the complaint is heard by either the regional superintendent or superintendent of schools.

Various approaches may be used by faculty members at any level of the educational system to deal with grievances. One common approach is that of silent acquiescence. This tactic is used because teachers may not want to risk being labelled as a "troublemaker" and possibly jeopardize potential salary raises, promotion, favorable assignments in course schedule and other responsibilities, and early tenure consideration. This approach, however, may not only prove frustrating to the teacher but, where the grievances have a factual basis and signify actual weaknesses in the educational system, using it will not actually rectify deficiencies that need to be overcome.

A second approach is to appeal through established channels and, after these channels have been exhausted, one accepts the decision, whether or not the ruling is in one's favor. This is the legalistic approach, an approach based on the conviction that further dissent after all formal grievance procedures had been utilized would set a bad example for others to follow. It is said that this is a nation of laws, not of men; to fly in the face of a duly-regulated system would tend ultimately to undermine it. One has so-to-speak had one's day in court and should rightfully abide by the decision. If everyone refused to abide by every policy with which they were dissatisfied, our institutions could not long remain intact and the benefits, protection, and continuity of institutional experience would be lost and most of us would be diminished.

Legal systems, however, pose serious problems because they do not inquire whether the distribution of a system of rights itself is just, since the law is not the judge of the norm it defines. The law establishes a distribution of rights as a normative equilibrium for society. It is what those who legislate have stipulated as the normal condition of society, which they would by law preserve, and if lost, by law restore. Thus, an independent evaluation of the quality of justice of a given legal system is an appropriate undertaking.

An alternative to such choices as silent acquiescence or appeal through established channels is to engage in furtive disobedience. This latter approach however, since it does not bring the abuses to public attention, will likely allow the abuses to go unchecked. Though furtive disobedience may temporarily alleviate some teachers' frustrations, it shows a lack of moral courage for refusal to publicly oppose abuses and is highly unlikely to provide lasting changes or benefits; rather, the probable administrative response would be greater restrictions and more severe sanctions once the culprits are apprehended.

Should, then, teachers resort to strikes to settle grievances and gain new demands? Resort to strikes has been increasingly employed. The number of work stoppages in local government increased rapidly from 42 in 1965 to 446 in 1975. This number leveled off briefly and rose to 536 in 1979, with 315 in education.[29]

All but eight states have a prohibition against strikes by public school teachers and other public employees as contrary to the public interest. Those eight states provide a modified right to strike after impasse resolution has been exhausted. Some of the remaining states have bargaining statutes and others do not. Of the former states, mediation, fact-finding, and arbitration are usually provided. Those states prohibiting strikes use injunctions to order strikers back to work.

The legal, professional, and ethical domains, however, do not always coincide. For instance, prior to the Brown decision in 1954 it was sanctioned by law in the deep South and some border states to have "separate but equal" school systems. It was professionally sanctioned as well and severe penalties were imposed on white teachers who led desegregation efforts. Moreover, professional educational organizations were segregated not only in those sections of the country but in some cases nationally. But despite legal and professional sanction of segregation, segregation was just as unethical before as after the Brown decision. With other issues—strikes, for instance—the legal, professional, and ethical may more closely coincide.

Mediation, fact-finding, and arbitration are, where provided in law, appeals through established channels and not a resort to civil disobedience. Once an impasse is reached, mediation and fact-finding are compulsory procedures. Compulsory arbitration as a final impasse step is currently required in three states. Where strikes are sanctioned, impasse procedures must be exhausted before a strike is permitted.

Are strikes unprofessional? As you may recall from Chapter One, professions are organized to provide a unique public social service: this means that they are organized to serve the public welfare as well as to foster their own interests by utilizing their professional skills. Professionals are expected to provide gratis service to the destitute and to adjust their fees with other impecunious individuals and families. Professionals at times may be expected to risk their lives or their reputation to fulfill obligations to individuals and/or serve the public welfare. But these responsibilities do not require professionals to take vows of poverty, with the exception that public school teaching and the ministry are two professions that usually pose financial hardships for its practitioners. One reason teaching is faced with this condi-

29. U.S. Department of Labor, Bureau of Labor Statistics: *Work Stoppages in Government, 1979.* Washington, D.C., U.S. Government Printing Office, 1981.

tion is the popular image of teacher: it is generally not considered a full-fledged profession.

Whether strikes are unprofessional would seem to hinge on whether they undermine the public welfare. Of course teachers have to be concerned with their own welfare, but where an act, though in the interest of teachers, runs counter to the public welfare, it would seem to be unprofessional (by the very nature of a profession). Of course it might be claimed that a professional person always obeys the law, in which case striking, where legally prohibited, would be unprofessional. But to make this claim suggests that teachers should have fewer civil rights than other citizens, viz., special restrictions on engaging in civil disobedience, and there does not seem to be any legal or moral basis for claiming teachers should be so disfranchised. Thus the argument relating professionalism and obligations to the public welfare is more plausible. In fact, professional and legal considerations coincide insofar as states which prohibit public employees from striking do so on the ground that such strikes are contrary to the public interest.

It is frequently contended that a strike is damaging to children and a threat to the public interest. However, it should be observed that schools are closed for the summer and holidays, for sports events, inclement weather, teachers' conventions and for other reasons without anyone becoming disturbed over harm done to children. Thus the alleged harm, except in protracted strikes, may be exaggerated. Nevertheless, strikes do violate laws and also may set an undesirable moral example; consequently, the grounds for a strike should be firm.

One thing that teachers could do if they believe that a strike in a particular case is morally justified is to help educate the public as to the reasons that brought about the strike, the nature of school conditions which they oppose, and explain that a work stoppage in the form of a strike will not have the dire consequences that the public has been led to believe. To secure social recognition of the moral rightness of a strike, teachers need to demonstrate that collective negotiations have been entered into in good faith but proved unsuccessful and that the educational conditions to which teachers and students are daily exposed are highly undesirable and have not been corrected even though they have repeatedly been brought to the attention of education authorities.

Thus before teachers can claim a moral justification for striking, they must first exhaust legal devices for redress of grievances and call to public attention more dramatically by striking those conditions which are not in the public interest. In other words, because teachers claim to be professionals, then the thrust of their work is to serve the public interest, even though at times teachers' interests may overlap if not coincide with those of the public. Most frequently strikes are initiated for higher teacher salaries and better

working conditions rather than insufficient per pupil expenditures, violations of academic freedom of teachers and students, unsafe schools, and other
serious deficiencies that one could likely make a case are in the public
interest to rectify. Union representatives should show that the satisfaction of
teachers' material demands will also have a positive effect on student achievement and/or improve the learning environment for teachers and students.

Those states which prohibit strikes by public employees are saying that
ipso facto strikes are not in the public interest. The point here, however, is
that whereas some strikes may be morally justified, others are not justifiable
and cannot be rendered morally acceptable. What would likely occur if
strikes were evaluated on a case-by-case basis is that a number of teacher
strikes could not be morally justified and teachers and teacher unions would
be penalized for engaging in them; others would be found morally justifiable and, consequently, school boards would be expected to rectify conditions and fulfill teacher demands in such cases. If such a plan were operative,
teacher unions would be more cautious in strike deliberations and more
careful in formulating the moral grounds for engaging in any given strike.

DISMISSAL, TENURE, RETRENCHMENT, AND RETIREMENT

Teachers can be dismissed for incompetence, immorality, insubordination,
unprofessional conduct, and economic reasons. Distinctions in handling
dismissal are made between tenured teachers and those in a probationary
period, though both groups are expected to enjoy academic freedom. The
AAUP holds that each faculty member should be given precise terms and
conditions of appointment and informed early in his or her appointment of
the substantive and procedural standards used in determining contract renewal and the granting of tenure.[30] Provision should be made for periodic
review of faculty member's progress, and she should be given an opportunity to submit material that will aid in making such evaluations. Notice of
nonreappointment should be given not later than March 1 of the first
academic year of service; not later than December 15 of the second academic
year; and at least twelve months in advance after two or more years in the
institution.[31] If a nontenured faculty member's contract is not renewed, she
should be informed in writing and, if she so requests reasons for the decision,
should be so advised. She can also request a reconsideration of the decision.[32]
Termination for cause against a tenured faculty member or one whose term

---

30. AAUP: Statement of procedural standards in the renewal or nonrenewal of faculty appointments. In
AAUP *Policy Documents and Reports*, pp. 8–12.

31. Academic freedom and tenure: 1970 interpretive comments. Ibid., p. 4.

32. Statement on procedural standards. Ibid., p. 2.

appointment has not expired should provide the faculty member due process and, if possible, it should be considered by a faculty committee and the governing board of the institution. The accused should have an opportunity to be informed in writing of the charges against him, have an opportunity to be heard in his own defense and be assisted by legal counsel.[33]

Some salient differences are found in the public schools. Public school teachers have a shorter probationary period: on the average three years rather than up to seven years (as in higher education). And in public schools notification of termination is not usually given as far in advance as the AAUP recommends for higher education. But the NEA has prescribed that superintendents provide a written statements of reasons for terminating a contract or nonrenewal of a contract when requested by the teacher.[34]

Returning to the principle of justice enunciated earlier in the chapter, one cannot make distinctions among teachers or among administrators without relevant reasons. When faculty members are given a statement of the precise terms of employment, the standards for merit and promotion, and are provided an opportunity to submit materials for promotion deliberations, the outward procedural processes are being properly followed. Yet even within these procedures it is possible for a committee to recommend dismissal on irrelevant grounds—race, sex, ethnicity, or religion—but claim other grounds for the decision. Thus this would be an example of invidious discrimination. In tenure hearings the irrelevant grounds are likely to be uncovered.

Tenured teachers can only be dismissed for cause. Among the grounds for dismissal mentioned earlier—incompetency and insubordination—are grounds where relevant reasons may be evident. To establish insubordination, it must be shown that the teacher deliberately violated a reasonable school rule that is understandable. The teacher must willfully violate the school rule, not inadvertently or by carelessness. Rules which violate the teachers civil rights, such as First Amendment rights to free speech, are invalid.[35]

Among the legal grounds for judging a teacher incompetent are a lack of knowledge of one's subject, physical disability that seriously impairs teaching, and mental disability (e.g., serious mental illness), and inability to maintain discipline.[36] Thus, once any of these grounds can be established, relevant reasons are available for discharging the teacher. One recent controversy is over the use of written competency tests, which some claim discriminate

---

33. Academic freedom and tenure. Ibid., p. 2.

34. NEA: *Opinions of the Committee on Professional Ethics*, opinion 36, p. 66.

35. Fischer, Louis, Schimmel, David, and Kelly, Cynthia: *Teachers and The Law.* New York, Longman, 1981, pp. 18–20.

36. Ibid., pp. 20–23.

against blacks and various ethnic groups because their failure rate is generally higher than Anglos. It is doubtful, however, that a written competence test, which a significant portion of the test may comprise problems in mathematics and language skills rather than strictly test for a knowledge of one's subject, is a relevant reason for rendering a final judgment about teacher competence. Such tests and other measures, along with objective evidence of actual teaching ability, would be needed. Moreover, since competency tests are required by law today in many states, then it behooves school systems, as a matter of fairness, to provide faculty development programs to help teachers improve their scores.

Tenure, Retrenchment, and Retirement

With the decline of opportunities for a career in academia—especially in the humanities, fine arts, and the social sciences—young Ph.D.'s may opt for a modification of tenure to remove what they believe to be an unfair encumbrance to their career aspirations. Criticisms against tenure can also be found in the literature, and some administrators and state legislatures have attacked tenure and sought to institute plans which would either modify or abolish it. This concern about tenure has arisen largely from the press of retrenchment that began in the 1970s and a concomitant reassessment of faculty.

Attacks on tenure have recently come from various locales and sources. Governor Richard D. Lamm said that Colorado colleges and schools should consider eliminating faculty tenure, and that there should be longer probationary periods or a new policy of "renewable tenure."[37] Various professional organizations in Canada and abroad have urged William Bennett, premier of British Columbia, to withdraw legislation that would abolish academic tenure and permit dismissal of public employees without cause or due process.[38] The government of British Columbia, following widespread criticism, has softened such legislation and would permit termination for a limited number of reasons.[39] Tenure survived a major challenge at the University of Nevada when a code proposed by the regents was compromised after strenuous faculty objections. The code would have made tenure more difficult to gain and harder to keep, made it easier to terminate tenured faculty members, and could have required some professors to submit to

37. Colorado governor seeks re-examination of tenure. *The Chronicle of Higher Education, 27:* 3, August 3, 1983.

38. Faculty groups in four countries hit plan to abolish tenure in British Columbia. Ibid., p. 18.

39. British Columbia amends legislation that critics said threaten tenure. *The Chronicle of Higher Education, 27:* 25–6, August 31, 1983.

medical or psychiatric examinations.[40] The point is that tenure is under pressure today from various sources primarily because of retrenchment rather than fear of Communist subversion (as in the 1950s) or other causes.[41]

Some regents have proposed long-term renewable contracts of five years or more as an alternative to tenure. Critics have suggested using a free marketplace ideology for schools and colleges.[42] Whereas a different proposal is to employ professional sports as a model, with free agents, trading, and salary arbitration.[43] A different tack, since the proportion of tenured faculty is rising at many colleges and universities, is to impose tenure quotas.

With all the criticism of tenure, what is its justification? Tenure can be justified on three grounds. Tenure, first of all, provides job security, which may be an inducement to those tempted by the blandishments of higher salaries and generous perquisites of business and industry. Second, according to Parsons and Platt, the educational and socialization functions of the university require some pattern of stratification and competence and tenure is an element of that pattern of stratification.[44] Finally, tenure is designed to protect academic freedom.

The most common proposal for modifying tenure is to institute long-term renewable contracts or periodic reviews whereby the faculty member is systematically evaluated after a stipulated time period and her contract is either renewed or she is discharged. These proposed changes, however, may undermine academic freedom by pressuring professors to conform by avoiding controversial issues. Is insufficient evaluation actually the problem? Tenured faculty members have already undergone a rigorous probationary period unlike that of any other profession. Such contracts and periodic review may also lead to serious morale problems and make careers in higher education less attractive. Many kinds of evaluations already occur for merit pay, research support, and teaching awards; these are evaluations of tenured faculty, but not in the sense of what is proposed in renewable contracts. Such contracts or any other system where colleges decide repeatedly whether to retain a professor is a form of term tenure, which is an oxymoron. Colleges and universities can use faculty development programs to help improve

40. Ill will remains at U. of Nevada after tenure truce. *The Chronicle of Higher Education,* 26I: 5–6, June 15, 1983.

41. For earlier tenure issues, see: Byse, Clark and Joughin, Louis: *Tenure in American Higher Education.* Ithaca, Cornell University Press, 1959.

42. O'Toole, J.: *Tenure: Three Views.* New Rochelle, N.Y., Change Magazine Press, 1979.

43. Divorkin, J. B. and Johnson, R. W.: A sporting alternative to tenure. *Bulletin of American Association of University Professors, 69,* 41–45, February 1979.

44. Parsons, Talcott and Platt, Gerald M.: *The American University.* Cambridge, Mass., Harvard University Press, 1973, pp. 364–65.

competencies, and institutions can promote a more supportive environment for teaching and research. As for incompetent tenured professors, mechanisms are already available for discipline and dismissal.

But is the present system in the best interest of educational institutions and fair to nontenured faculty? Doctoral programs throughout the nation multiplied during the years of burgeoning enrollments in the 1960s and most faculties were averse to cutbacks but some were forced to do so during the 1970s. This lack of prescience and selfregulation by directors of graduate programs created an oversupply of fresh Ph.D.'s in some disciplines, a disenchanted group that had vainly aspired to an academic career and had to retool themselves for different careers than initially envisioned.

This problem, though belatedly, is being rectified. The total number of doctorates granted by U.S. universities declined from an all-time high of 33,146 in 1975 to 30,982 in 1980. And there has also been a shift in the number of Ph.D.s in various disciplines. Since 1974, the number of Ph.D.s awarded in the humanities has decreased dramatically.[45]

Yet it should be noted that a tenure decision is about a 30-year contract that costs the institution, apart from other commitments, from $400,000 to $1 million in salary alone. Academic salaries are the largest part of the college budget and are least amenable to short-run reduction.[46] These figures, however, are somewhat deceptive insofar as the contract is not actually for 30 years in view of faculty turnover, some of the costs are borne extramurally through research grants, the contract is not as expensive as it appears in view of inflation, and those who fail to gain tenure at one university may receive it later at another.[47]

But as retrenchment deepened in the late 1970s, some administrators and regents called for tenure quotas as being in the institution's best interest. The AAUP policy statement opposes tenure quotas on several grounds.[48] A numerical quota system indefensibly extends conditions which jeopardize academic freedom by obviating the evaluation of affected individuals on their academic record. It therefore places those who have fully earned, but not received, tenure in a less favorable and more vulnerable position than tenured colleagues, and institutes a probationary system that is not actually probation but probation that leads to automatic termination. The tenure system should not be compromised by administrative desire for convenience

---

45. U.S. Department of Education, National Center of Education Statistics, *Digest of Education Statistics,* 1980.

46. Cohen, Michael D. and March, James G.: *Leadership and Ambiguity: The American College President.* New York, McGraw-Hill, 1974, p. 108.

47. Ibid., pp. 109–10

48. On the imposition of tenure quotas. AAUP *Policy Documents and Reports,* pp. 23–25.

and flexibility. Instead the AAUP alternatives for greater equity and improved morale are for institutions not to be alarmed by a temporary increase in the percentage of tenured faculty members, initiate accelerated retirement opportunities for senior faculty, and plan more effectively the proportion of teaching and research of full-time and part-time tenured and probationary faculty.

In addition to the AAUP statement other points should be considered. Periods of retrenchment should mobilize faculty in planning to make certain that the administration does not declare financial exigency prematurely, that retrenchment is bonafide and demonstrable and not a ruse for eliminating unpopular programs or unpopular faculty members. Guidelines need to be developed by faculty and administration prior to financial exigencies to avert these abuses and to prevent those who perceive their programs as threatened from urging the elimination of someone else's program. One way the latter problem could be avoided is that once a budget committee questions the need for a program, the final decision about the program should rest with the faculty senate or a policy-making body sensitive to university programs as a whole.

Some state laws provide that tenured teachers can be dismissed for economic reasons. Courts have held that, even where no relevant state law or contractual provision exists, school officials have the authority to dismiss teachers for economic reasons. The most common reasons for dismissal are decline in student enrollment, curriculum reorganization for economic reasons, and decisions to abolish a particular position based on economy and not the result of prejudice or discrimination.[49]

The AAUP's guidelines for financial exigency also affirms the importance of meaningful faculty participation in such decisions.[50] Those whose programs are likely to be affected should be heard. Tenured professors, according to the AAUP, should not be terminated in favor of nontenured professors who at a particular moment seem to be more productive. Criteria used in termination should include age and length of service. Tenured faculty should be given an opportunity to readapt within the department or elsewhere within the institution. Earlier retirement may be feasible for older tenured faculty by the institution investing additional funds in the individual's retirement income.

What the AAUP seems to have in mind in retaining the tenured professor over the nontenured, more productive one is the protection of academic freedom. It also implies that declaring financial exigency is not the way to

---

49. Fischer, et al.: *Teachers and the Law,* pp. 39–42.

50. On institutional problems resulting from financial exigency: Some operating guidelines. AAUP *Policy Documents and Reports,* pp. 48–49.

eliminate unpopular or unproductive professors. But "unproductive" does not necessarily mean "incompetent"; perhaps "unproductive" needs to be defined operationally. However, if it is a synonymn for incompetence, then incompetence is a legal ground for dismissal and the AAUP's point is therefore invalid.

Other recommendations for faculty in financial exigencies is that they should be involved in preexigency planning, resist unfounded administrative attempts to declare states of exigency, develop careful guidelines to handle retrenchment, and accept a proper share of responsibility for determining necessary terminations.[51]

Retirement decisions are not only of interest in retrenchment but in terms of equity and fairness to faculty members involved. Mandatory retirement at age 65 was abolished by the Age Discrimination in Employment Act Amendment of 1978 that became effective on January 1, 1979. The act, however, still permits mandatory retirement provisions at age 70. The Supreme Court had earlier upheld retirement statues if there was a reasonable connection between the law and a legitimate state interest such as opening up places for minorities, providing greater opportunities for younger faculty, and providing greater predictability in administering pension plans.[52]

But if the object is to provide more places for minorities and younger teachers, then raising the mandatory age from 65 to 70 is not the way to accomplish it. However, if the arguments used against mandatory retirement at 65 are valid, they are also valid for age 70. Mandatory retirement at age 65, it was claimed, is arbitrary and age alone is a poor indication of ability; thus mandatory retirement is a poor method for eliminating incompetent and unproductive teachers. Older workers also have good records of low absenteeism, dependability, and work quality.

Returning to the principle of justice stated earlier, one cannot make distinctions without relevant reasons; it does not appear that age alone is a relevant reason to institute mandatory retirement. Such retirement plans seem to employ invidious discrimination unless it can be shown that most faculty members will become incompetent by age 70.

TIAA–CREF (a national pension plan for professors) mailed a questionnaire to 2,200 randomly selected annuitants asking them a wide range of questions about their retirement experiences; of these, 84 percent returned the questionnaires.[53] Ninety percent said they were satisfied with their

---

51. Strohm, Paul: Faculty responsibilities and rights during retrenchment. In Mingle, James R. and Associates. *Challenges of Retrenchment.* San Francisco, Jossey-Bass, 1981, p. 151.

52. Fischer, et al.: *Teachers and the Law,* pp. 227–28.

53. Teachers Insurance and Annuity Association: *The Participant.* New York, The Association, August 1983.

retirement. Sixty-six percent retired by choice at the time they selected, and 34 percent did not retire by choice. Of the latter group, 6 percent became disabled or had poor health; 7 percent were forced out due to administration decisions, elimination of positions, and budget cuts; and 21 percent reached their employer's mandatory retirement age. Thus although some who were forced to retire had to do so before 70 but under present laws would no longer be penalized (though they still may be dissatisfied with mandatory retirement at any age), others may have been in institutions that do not require retirement until 70.

Thus two recommendations seem to be in order. Rather than mandatory retirement at age 70, each faculty member should be judged on a case-by-case basis. The substitution of one-year renewable contracts for tenured professors at age 70 rather than mandatory retirement is unsatisfactory because it does not sufficiently protect academic freedom. Second, in order to open more faculty positions, retirement could be made more attractive and accessible by educational institutions collaborating with outside insurance agencies to develop plans to enable faculty members who are interested in early retirement to lay aside funds that will allow them to fulfill their decision without facing considerable financial hardships. Judging by the TIAA–CREF survey of retirees, a range of attitudes toward retirement can be found. Of the 66 percent who retired by choice and at the time they selected, 10 percent viewed current employment as no longer desirable or suitable, 42 percent sought retirement as an attractive alternative to current employment, and 14 percent retired for a variety of reasons.[54] Probably a number of these retirees would have taken advantage of early retirement if it had been available to them. Thus early retirement options will provide older faculty members greater alternatives and more satisfaction with their retirement plans and open up new positions and opportunities for minorities and younger faculty; at the same time, invidious discrimination will be eliminated by abolishing mandatory retirement provisions and judging those who reach age 70 on a case-by-case basis, similarly to the way decisions are currently made about tenured faculty when considered for merit raises, promotion, grants, and awards.

---

54. Ibid.

Chapter Seven

THE EDUCATOR IN THE COMMUNITY

Teacher behavior in the community has long been under scrutiny. In a society undergoing rapid transformation not only in its material culture but also in its values and beliefs, the roles of educators and other professional groups are undergoing significant changes. Schools and colleges interact with the larger society and thereby are subject to their influences and changing conditions. These transformations—particularly those that signify a change in values and ideals—affect the responsibilities and roles of the teacher. Dramatic alterations in the family, the shift from a rural to an industrial and then a postindustrial nation, strong labor movements that recruit teachers, and the rapid growth of centralized government have all had a significant impact on education.

This chapter is concerned, first of all, with the rights and responsibilities of the educator as a citizen. Thus this chapter inquires not only about present expectations for educators but how they were formerly treated in order that the reader may better understand today's problems and changed conditions. Should there be special standards for teachers in their communities (as opposed to other professionals and to laypersons)? Also explored are the restrictions and obligations of teachers who seek public office. A second major area of concern are the criteria for community misconduct and the grounds for dismissal. Finally, an investigation is made of teachers' relations with parents and the professional responsibilities and obligations involved.

RIGHTS AND RESPONSIBILITIES OF EDUCATORS AS CITIZENS

Teachers in Colonial America were expected to be loyal to the civil government, religiously orthodox, and morally acceptable.[1] As the colonies were subject to the rule of England, teachers and other officials were expected to be loyal to the mother country and demonstrate it by taking a loyalty oath. The schoolmaster was also expected to exhibit the proper religious views and practices consonant with the dominant religion of the particular colony. The matter of moral character, frequently construed as

---

1. Butts, R. Freeman and Cremin, Lawrence A.: *A History of Education in American Culture.* New York, Holt, 1953, pp. 131–132.

prohibitions from certain actions rather than a clearly conceived positive system of morality, was a matter of close surveillance not only during colonial times but up to the present day. This moral code was usually more orthodox and restrictive than citizens of the community, other than clergy, observed. Largely through the history of American education individuals recruited for teaching were those who would likely abide by such codes. "Few teachers," according to Beale, "had ever thought of differing from colonial views. Most regarded themselves as guardians of correct thinking."[2]

Although during the nineteenth century teacher preparation was placed for the first time on a systematic basis, the restrictions imposed upon teachers scarcely diminished despite higher qualifications. The use of tobacco and liquor was stringently regulated, with the use of the latter always grounds for dismissal from teaching. Gambling and profane language were also taboo; and it was expected, especially in smaller communities, that teachers would attend church regularly and participate in religious activities. Whereas for people in the community, on the other hand, it was a common practice in the mid-nineteenth century for men to chew tobacco and for men and women of higher social classes to drink at social gatherings; gambling, in various forms, was also widespread. The single teacher's dating behavior was usually carefully observed—and in some communities forbidden; in other cases, restrictions were imposed in terms of the time that teachers should be in at night. Prudery grew during the Victorian period: nude statues were clothed or barred altogether; reference could not be made to the word "leg" in mixed company; and one girl's school draped piano legs.[3]

As the qualifications of teachers continued to improve in the nineteenth century, less complaints were registered about improper conduct even though restrictions were great throughout the Victorian era (1837–1901). Since most teachers came from families who extolled community standards, the vast majority of teachers willingly complied with community demands.

The professor's background differed from the public school teacher. Prior to the Civil War, the professor was frequently a clergyman or had some theological training. But the clergyman was not as esteemed as the squire, the lawyer-politician, the man of affairs, who was embroiled in American life rather than apart from it as was the clergyman-professor. This separation from practical affairs would not recommend the professor to his students or to the students' fathers. Rarely were professors of this period scholars; they were concerned with promoting moral rec-

---

2. Beale, Howard K.: *A History of Freedom of Teaching in American Schools.* New York, Scribner's, 1941, p. 38.

3. Ibid., p. 106.

titude and Christian values through liberal education.[4]

From 1862 to 1910 American higher education was transformed in several major ways. Liberal education expanded its scope from strictly classical and religious studies. The older classicists who conceived their task as building moral character and mental discipline were eschewed; the formal discipline theory was coming under severe attack. The outcomes of liberal culture were instead extolled in such phrases as "breadth of learning and understanding," "sensibility and artistic feeling," and "serenity and solidity of mind."[5] The student would be expected to combine broad learning with aesthetic tastes and moral development. A study of literary models and philosophical works, rather than reliance upon religion, were used to contribute to character development. Thus the professor as secular humanist replaced the clergyman.

The other two major changes were the development of the research university and the emergence of applied and technological studies. The research university, modelled on the nineteenth century German university, arose in the 1870s and led to the growth of graduate programs, basic scientific research, and the professor as researcher.

Applied and technological studies grew with the Morrill Act of 1862, which initiated the land grant movement that provided agricultural and mechanical colleges. The former criticism of the clergyman-professor as divorced from the world of everyday affairs would no longer apply to the new professor who related to local communities through applied knowledge in agriculture, home economics, social work, and business. Professors became practical men who could grapple with the diverse and persistent problems of everyday life.

Changes in community attitudes toward public school teachers came about with industrialization and the migration of large numbers of people to cities. Homogeneity of communities began to break down with the growth of urbanization, and some of the older standards began to erode as a result of the first world war. Accompanying these changes was a growing secularization of culture and a willingness to entertain a scientific world view. Modern science and critical studies of Biblical texts began to shake the religious faith of some urban dwellers.

One of the most salient changes since the 1930s has been the transformation in the type of communities in which the majority of American teachers live. Most teachers during the 1930s lived in small towns and rural areas,

---

4. Rudolph, Frederick: *The American College and University: A History.* New York, Vintage Books, 1962, pp. 157–161.

5. Veysey, Laurence R.: *The Emergence of the American University.* Chicago, University of Chicago Press, 1965, p. 186.

what sociologists have called "sacred" or folk communities. Today the majority of teachers live in large urban areas.

A prominent characteristic of teachers today is their greater heterogeneity. More teachers today than in the past will protest grievances, bring suits, strike, engage in sanctions and other militant activities. It is difficult for citizens who accept the traditional image of teachers to reconcile their thinking with the actualities of teacher militancy.

Are there reasons for having special community standards for teachers? For instance, ministers may unofficially be expected to observe higher moral standards and a more circumscribed life than members of their congregation, whereas other professionals are usually not subjected to double standards, except occasionally in some small communities.

The NEA's Bill of Teacher Rights states that teachers have the right to express their views publicly about education. Teachers should enjoy all the basic constitutional rights: freedom of speech, religion, assembly, association, political action, and equal protection of the law.[6]

In contrast, the AAUP takes a different position by ostensibly establishing a special standard for professors to observe in the community. In its famous 1940 statement on academic freedom and tenure—which has since been endorsed by dozens of scholarly organizations—the AAUP held that since the public may judge the profession by the professor's utterances, he should "at all times be accurate, should exercise appropriate restraint, should show respect for the opinions of others, and should make every effort to indicate that he is not an institutional spokesman."[7]

But when we come to the AAUP Statement on Professional Ethics (formulated in 1966), the professor is urged to avoid conveying the impression when speaking as a private citizen that he speaks for his institution, but no mention is made of other responsibilities in the 1940 Statement. He also has an obligation to promote free inquiry and public understanding of academic freedom.[8] Here it is not clear whether academic freedom is conceived in a more restrictive view as institutional freedom in teaching and research or the more encompassing but problematic view as emerging from the civil rights all citizens enjoy.

In 1964 the AAUP issued a new statement on extramural utterances that averred that the professor's community expression cannot be grounds for dismissal unless it can be clearly demonstrated through an appropriate

---

6. Bill of teacher rights. In NEA *Handbook 1979-80.* Washington, D.C., The Association, 1979, pp. 283–84.

7. Academic freedom and tenure. In American Association of University Professors: *Policy Documents and Reports.* Washington, D.C., The Association, 1977, p. 2.

8. Statement on Professional Ethics. Ibid., p. 66.

faculty hearing committee. But the statement added that such utterances rarely relate to competency, and any final decision should consider the faculty member's entire record as scholar and teacher.[9]

Thus the AAUP seems to have backtracked on its 1940 statement and adopted a wiser position. It would appear to be "wiser" because the 1940 statement (as it pertains to this issue) carries no ethical weight, as it contradicts the professor's civil liberties by establishing a special standard without demonstrating overriding grounds for supporting the position. Of course it would be prudential to be accurate, exercise restraint, and the like because presumably as a learned person the professor has the ability to do so and it would therefore set a favorable example where public dialogue had heretofore been intemperate and inaccurate. But there can be no ethical obligation unless it could be demonstrated that failure to follow the 1940 guidelines violates professional obligations. The 1940 AAUP Statement on extramural utterances seems to be a case of supererogation.

A community activity that has been subject to considerable restriction is that of engaging in political activity and running for political office. Some colleges and universities prohibit holding political office, managing political campaigns, and related activities; whereas other institutions merely request that faculty members inform their administration about these activities. Restrictions on political activity, which emanate from institutional regulations and state legislation, vary greatly from one university to another.

The AAUP holds that the professor, as a citizen, should be free to engage in political activity so long as it does not interfere with his or her professional obligations. Since these are legitimate and socially important activities, institutional arrangements should be made in the form of a reduced workload or a leave of absence. The AAUP adds that such leaves may create problems for one's administration or colleagues and he should not abuse the *privilege* by overly frequent or late applications or too extended a leave. The terms of the leave and its effect on the professor's status should be stated in writing; the leave should not affect tenure consideration other than it need not count as probationary service.[10]

To place an absolute prohibition on political activities or to require professors to resign should they become a candidate for political office denies them their citizenship rights. Of course the faculty member's institution has the legitimate authority to determine the timing and the length of the leave to avoid unnecessary hardship on programs and colleagues. These political activities, while they are citizenship rights, cannot be as freely exercised as one who is selfemployed or retired. It is not, however, a "privilege"

---

9. Committee A statement on extramural utterances. Ibid., p. 14.

10. Statement on professors and political activity. Ibid., pp. 26–27.

as the AAUP construes it, since it is not a right or immunity attached specifically to a position or an office. The notion of privilege applies to a special right that is granted as a favor or concession or belongs to someone as a prerogative; it usually implies an advantage over others. Thus an educator's political activity is a right that needs to be exercised under reasonable restraint; and by 'reasonable' is meant that so long as one holds a professional position the first obligation is to that position; consequently, the faculty member will not insist on a leave of absence or use large amounts of time in political activities if it interferes with his professional responsibilities or undermines the academic program to which he is originally committed.

COMMUNITY MISCONDUCT AND GROUNDS FOR DISMISSAL

Earlier it was noted that teachers can legally be fired for incompetence, insubordination, immorality, and unprofessional conduct. Though the importance of privacy, especially in connection with research with human subjects, was discussed earlier, teachers may not expect legal protection of privacy in their personal lives because privacy is a newly evolving constitutional freedom that has not been adequately tested by the courts. This lack of protection is unfortunate in light of the history of surveillance over teachers' private lives, a condition that has only partly abated in recent years.

Courts have varied in their interpretations of alleged immorality in the community, but generally court decisions depend upon the circumstances of the case and whether the activity has or is likely to have a negative influence on teaching. Courts might consider the notoriety of the activity, when it took place (prior to employment in the school district or while employed in the district), and whether it occurred in the local community where employed. Also considered by some courts is whether the behavior sets a bad example with students. For instance, a school board might contend that a teacher's repeated arrests for intoxication sets a bad example for the school's educational program to discourage alcoholism. Judges, according to Fischer, would likely say that the negative impact is obvious in the use of illegal drugs, drunk driving, and armed assault; but whether the negative impact is great in being a homosexual, committing a felony, or being an unwed mother would depend upon the circumstances.[11] Various state courts, for example, have ruled differently on homosexual behavior of teachers: some courts ruled that teachers could not be dismissed for such conduct unless it related to their professional work; whereas other courts have upheld dismissal when the teacher admitted to a school official that he was a homosexual. A school

---

11. Fischer, Louis, Schimmel, David, and Kelly, Cynthia: *Teachers and the Law.* New York, Longman, 1981, ch. 13.

may be able to dismiss a single teacher who visibly becomes pregnant during the school year but not one who had a child out of wedlock in the past.

Courts, at one time or another, have considered the following teacher conduct immoral: homosexuality, unwed mothers, sexual advances toward students, talking to students about sex when it is not related to the curriculum, excessive drinking, commission of a felony, possessing illegal drugs, using vulgar or "obscene" language with students, and other grounds. Are all of these activities actually immoral and thereby grounds for dismissal of both probationary and tenured teachers? Some of these activities? If so, which ones? What are the grounds for selection? All of these activities but only under certain circumstances? What, then, are the circumstances and limiting conditions?

The notion of immorality is a complex one because it involves understanding what it means to be moral. One way that this idea can be made clear is by distinguishing certain basic terms. First of all, the terms "mores" and "morality" should be distinguished. By *mores* is meant the fixed morally-binding customs of a particular group. Mores vary considerably cross-culturally and throughout human history, ranging from the noblest behavior to the approval of slavery, infanticide, burning infidels at the stake, genocide, and other practices. In contrast, *morality* is a system of moral conduct based on moral principles. That which is *moral*, therefore, relates to principles of right conduct in behavior; the behavior conforms to accepted principles of what is considered right, virtuous, or just. To say that a certain act is *immoral* means that it is unvirtuous or contrary to morality because it does not conform to principles of right conduct.

Two cognate terms should be considered: "amoral" and "nonmoral." *Amoral* has more than one meaning insofar as it may refer to someone who is indifferent to or does not care to abide by moral codes. Or it may refer to someone who lacks moral sensibility, such as infants, because of immaturity. It may also be equated with *nonmoral*, an act which is neither moral nor immoral, such as a decision to buy a particular tie.

The study of the nature of morality consists of two major approaches: the scientific and the philosophical. The scientific utilizes social science methodology to uncover how people actually behave and what they believe about morality. The philosophical approach, in contrast, is known as *ethics*, which is an inquiry into the nature of morality and moral acts. Ethics is divided into normative ethics and metaethics. Normative ethics is concerned with what people ought to do (Should one act in her own self-interest?) and studies systems of ethics (Epicureanism, Stoicism, Kantianism, utilitarianism, etc.). Metaethics analyzes ethical language and the justification of ethical inquiry and judgments.

Whereas manners are concerned with matters of taste and etiquette based on prudential judgments, morality concerns how humans treat other beings in order to promote their mutual welfare and the good life. Ethics is concerned with such concepts as "good," "right," and "ought."

In order to say that someone in a particular instance acted morally is meaningful only when an act is voluntary, intentional, based on moral principles, and considers the good of everyone likely to be affected by the act. It must be voluntary rather than coerced, intentional rather than accidental, based on sound reasons for the moral principle used, employ appropriate principles for the situation, and the agent considers the good of everyone affected by the act rather than his own good exclusively.

The agent must be able to be held responsible for the act before praise or blame can be ascribed or sanctions imposed. If the person is coerced, then responsibility cannot be assigned to that person; or if she accidentally commits an undesirable act, less responsibility can be assigned than if the act is intentional (though the person can be reprimanded for being careless in acts with untoward effects and not be given credit for accidental acts that have beneficial effects). As for moral principles, obviously someone who impulsively performs an act that has a beneficial effect on others cannot be considered to be demonstrating good moral character as would someone whose actions that are clearly guided by moral principles that are not arbitrarily chosen and are applied correctly to differing situations. The agent should also consider how her acts affect others, the possible benefits derived and the harm imposed. But no simple formula is available: one cannot merely quantify benefits and harms, as a serious harm to two people may be more morally undesirable than an act that slightly harms 50 people. For instance, an arsonist who totally destroys a family's home and possessions has committed a greater wrong than a bus driver who, through orneriness, keeps 50 people waiting ten minutes and causes some to be late for appointments. By "harm" is meant an injury to something in which a person has a genuine stake. Those things which one has a genuine stake are both permanent (one's health and security) and temporary (a piece of property that one plans to sell).

Thus when we look back at those acts which some communities consider immoral—homosexuality, unwed mothers, excessive drinking, commission of a felony, possessing illegal drugs, using vulgar or obscene language with students—it is not clear that they are immoral when the above criteria are applied. Some may clearly be unprofessional, such as using vulgar and obscene language with students; and teachers who have sexual relations with minor students seem to be engaged in illegal, immoral, and unprofessional acts. But sexual relations between teachers and consenting adult students are neither illegal nor immoral but unprofessional. The other acts listed above would appear to be not immoral but offensive to community members and seen by some citizens as setting an undesirable example for students.

Two tests could be used: Does the act seriously impair the teacher's effectiveness in fulfilling expected professional responsibilities? Does the act set an undesirable example for students? It would appear that most of the enumerated acts do not impair teacher effectiveness at least in a technical sense of efficiency, but some acts may, in the eyes of the community, set a bad example for impressionable students. But if the latter allegation is made, it behooves the school board to show clearly that the teacher's undesirable community behavior is well-known to students, the teacher has previously served as a model for student behavior, and students are beginning to model the undesirable behavior and/or their attitudes toward the undesirable behavior are beginning to become favorable where once they were indifferent or unfavorable. Unless these conditions could be demonstrated, the school board does not have clear grounds for discharging the teacher. Additionally, where the immorality of the act is debatable, the school board should forewarn teachers upon initial employment about the sanctions imposed for such acts so that teachers who plan to engage in such acts can seek employment in a district that does not consider the act immoral or else refrain from engaging in the disapproved acts should they decide to accept a position in the disapproving school district.

TEACHERS' RELATIONS WITH PARENTS

Elementary and secondary teachers have frequent relations with the parents of students; whereas at the college level such relations are infrequent because the student is considered independent and no longer a minor. The professor's relations with alumni are usually infrequent and sporadic, except in the case of former students. But what are the professional responsibilities of teachers toward parents, and how do these responsibilities relate to educational services?

It would appear that the nexus of parent-teacher relations would be the impact of the educational process on the child, both at home and school, except for the fact that parents are more generally engaged in socialization than education. Socialization is the process by which an individual acquires knowledge, skills, and behavior that will make him an adequate member of society. In the process one learns appropriate roles for his age, sex, social class, and personal responsibilities. The chief socializing influences in the nuclear family during preschool years would, first of all, be the parents, and secondarily, siblings, playmates, relatives, and the media.

Parenting is caught up with socialization processes that instill social roles and proper social rules that help preserve social institutions. Education, on the other hand, is usually designed to change and improve individuals and society by providing requisite knowledge and reflective abilities. This is less true in the early grades in which the acquisition of skills and a rudimentary knowledge of the cultural heritage are emphasized. This is not to say that the home fails to exercise an educative function; the point is that the family is primarily a socializing and nurturing institution whereas schools continue socialization but strive to be primarily an education institution. Thus the socialization process would appear to be the initial point where parents and teachers could more readily communicate about the child's schooling.

Interestingly, neither the latest NEA Code of Ethics nor the NEA Bill of Teacher Rights adopted in 1973 says anything about parent-teacher relationships, although the initial NEA Code of Ethics does offer some planks on this topic. The precise reasons why this section was deleted is open to speculation; however, the several revisions of the Code since 1952 involved widespread participation by the membership (which will be discussed in the next chapter).

The AASA Code of Ethics does state the obligation of school administrators to the community. The school administrator has an obligation to interpret both favorable and unfavorable activities of the school system to local citizens; it is unethical to present only favorable information to citizens.[12] This precept recognizes that the superintendent is a public servant who should understand that the best way to improve schools and to gain needed public support is to provide accurate information about activities and programs. Thus the superintendent does not put up a false front to make administrators and faculty artificially look good or to make his or her job more secure.

The 1952 version of the NEA Code of Ethics recognized that teachers and parents share responsibility for the learner, and that the teacher's effectiveness is dependent upon cooperative relationships with the home.[13] In fulfilling this obligation, the teacher should respect the parents' responsibility for their children; establish cooperative and friendly relations with the home; promote the student's confidence in his home and avoid disparaging remarks that may diminish that confidence; provide parents with information that will serve the interest of their children, and be discreet in handling such information; and, finally, keep parents informed about their children's progress as viewed in light of the school's purposes.

Prior to 1974, student records in some places were open to government inspectors, employers, and nonschool personnel but not to parents. In that year Congress passed the Family Educational Rights and Privacy Act (also

---

12. American Association of School Administrators. *The AASA Code of Ethics*. Washington, D.C., The Association, 1966, Policy 9A, p. 32.

13. NEA Code of Ethics. In *Opinions of the Committee on Professional Ethics*. Washington, D.C., The Association, 1956, Principle II, pp. 58–59.

known as the Buckley Amendment), which require school districts to develop a policy of how parents can inspect student records and inform parents of their rights under the act. The confidentiality of student records is protected by requiring parental permission before the records can be shared with outsiders. It also establishes procedures by which parents can challenge questionable information in the records.

But the FERPA contains no procedures for monitoring implementation or assuring compliance by local school districts. Although federal funds can be cut off if compliance cannot be voluntarily obtained, there is no obligation for the Department of Education to monitor abuses and no requirement for the state to report compliance.

To reduce the dangers inherent in abuses of cumulative records, the records should pertain to educational decision-making and exclude personal matters about sexual development, friendships, personal characteristics, and home stability. It may be necessary to limit the content of the records to the bare minimum.

In addition to the problem of handling information about students properly, one source of difficulty in gaining cooperative relationships between teachers and parents is the phenomenon of "boundary maintenance." This phenomenon refers to procedures used to separate those within the system from those outside the system. The stronger the school's boundaries, the less participation by parents in school affairs. In a study of 40 schools, it was found that parent-teacher interaction declined with formalization of school rules, centralization of decision-making, and solidarity of teacher organizations.[14]

Schools and families are engaged in complementary tasks, according to one observer, but find themselves in sharp conflict with one another.[15] The ideal parent from the teacher's viewpoint is one who accepts the teacher's expertise, shows appreciation for the teacher's efforts, gets the child to obey the teacher, and accepts blame for the child's weaknesses. The ideal teacher from the parents' perspective recognizes the child's special aptitudes and abilities, develops these so the child moves to or near the top of the class, and recognizes that the child's best qualities were inherited from the parents.[16]

Parents can become more involved in their children's education in any one or more of several roles: as an audience, as a teacher at home, as a school

14. Corwin, R. G. and Wagenaar, T. C.: Boundary interaction between service organizations and their publics: A study of teacher-parent relationships. *Social Forces, 55*(2), 471–491, 1976.

15. Lightfoot, Sara Lawrence: *Worlds Apart.* New York, Basic Books, 1978, p. 20.

16. Bredemeier, Mary E. and Bredemeier, Harry C.: *Social Forces in Education.* Sherman Oaks, Calif., Alfred Publishing, 1978, p. 276.

aide, as a paid volunteer, and a decision maker.[17] Parents as audience is a familiar pattern, but this pattern could be improved by schools' communicating more effectively to parents and the larger public. The parent as teacher at home involves parent education and the contribution schools can make by providing information, guidance, and programs. The parent as a paid volunteer would pay parents to attend school to learn techniques for teaching their child. In contrast, by parents becoming school aides, teachers are relieved of routine tasks; parents learn first-hand about school operations; and teachers, by working more directly with parents, may change their attitudes toward them. As for parents' participating in decision making, most federal legislation since the early 1970s mandates citizen participation in terms of consulting and advising. There are about 14,000 district-wide Title I Parent Advisory Committees and 44,000 building committees with a total of almost 900,000 members; moreover, an additional 150,000 persons serve on Follow through, Head Start, and other groups.[18] Thus the machinery and techniques are available for fostering improved parent-teacher relations.

17. Gordon, Ira, J.: Toward a home-school partnership program. In Gordon, Ira J. and Breirogal, William F. (Eds.): *Building Effective Home-School Relationships.* Boston: Allyn and Bacon, 1976, ch. 1.

18. A review of mandated citizen participation can be found in Cunningham, Luvern L., et al.: *Improving Education in Florida: A Reassessment.* Tallahassee, Select Joint Committee on Public Schools, 1978, pp. 215–295.

Chapter Eight

DISSEMINATING, IMPLEMENTING, AND ENFORCING ETHICAL CODES

The ultimate effectiveness of a professional code is found in the daily practices of its members. Most all professions have some type of ethical codes, and some professions in the United States (law, medicine, and others) have had codes much earlier than those of educators. But the date of a code's inception is less important than how well the code is developed and what is done with it after its formulation. Some codes are not well developed—overly general or too narrowly specific, negligent of significant problems, and the like. Other codes, though they may be well developed, are not adequately enforced.

Our concern in this chapter is with the latter problem. Specifically, this chapter focuses on the dissemination, implementation, and enforcement of codes of ethics for educators. Substantial accomplishments have been made in the area of dissemination, but more needs to be done. Less sanguine, the areas of implementation and enforcement exhibit serious shortcomings despite diverse efforts of various individuals, groups, and associations.

DISSEMINATION

The first state code of ethics for teachers was adopted by the Georgia Education Association in 1896. Most other state associations have since followed suit, with most adoptions occurring from 1920 to 1930.[1] The codes urged teachers to cooperate with associates, uphold the child's welfare, and live by high standards. Some codes also suggested that teachers and administrators should have a hand in school policy development.[2]

In 1924 the NEA appointed a committee to develop a national code for teachers, and in 1929 their first code was adopted. Since then, major revisions have occurred in 1941, 1944, 1952, 1963, 1968, and 1975.

Some idea of the effectiveness of the NEA in disseminating their code of ethics can be gained by examining their activities during a recent time

---

1. Martin, Theodore Day: *Building a Teaching Profession.* Middletown, N.Y., Whitlock Press, 1957, p. 144.

2. Donley, Marshall O., Jr.: *Power to the Teacher: How America's Educators Became Militant.* Bloomington, Indiana University Press, 1976, p. 25.

period. In 1958–59, the NEA distributed materials (the Code, Opinions, NEA Code of Ethics Poster, and other materials on professional ethics). A copy of Opinions was sent to each student NEA chapter. The Association also aided in the interpretation of the Code by publishing one of the opinions in the NEA *Journal,* and participated in conferences with local and state association members.[3] These dissemination activities were usually regularly engaged in during the 1960s and 1970s. In addition, in 1960, the NEA published a *Quiz on Professional Ethics,* pamphlets for use by local education associations, and a guide for committees dealing with professional ethics. The Code was further interpreted in response to questions from the field, and an exploration was made with affiliated state associations about developing a single code of ethics. It was urged that the NEA Code be so revised that all affiliates could subscribe to it.[4] Almost 51,000 persons in 502 local affiliates participated in deliberations in 1961 concerning the need for a single code of ethics.[5]

Efforts to disseminate the Code did not abate, as over 500,000 copies of the Code were distributed in 1964.[6] The NEA Committee on Professional Ethics continued efforts in subsequent years to improve beginning teachers' understanding of the Code and also tried to develop greater lay awareness.[7]

Although the above sample of the NEA's dissemination activities indicates a systematic and concerted effort over a considerable period, little has been done by teacher educators and others in preservice and inservice teacher education programs. McMullen states that the deliberate and systematic instruction of teacher candidates for compliance with statutory professional ethics is without precedent. His study shows that adequate information exists to develop a curriculum for professional ethics in preservice teacher education.[8] Although his study was published in 1970, there is no evidence since then to show that the neglect of professional ethics has been rectified.

Constans recommends in his study that for inservice teachers wide use should be made of pamphlets, study guides, research reports, journal articles, films, film strips, and tapes. And for preservice teachers he recommends that

---

3. National Education Association of the United States: *Addresses and Proceedings.* Washington, D.C., The Association, Vol. 97, 1959, pp. 314–15.

4. Ibid., Vol. 98, 1960, pp. 342–43.

5. Ibid., Vol. 99, 1961, p. 130.

6. Ibid., Vol. 102, 1964, p. 353.

7. Ibid., Vol. 105, 1967, pp. 425–27.

8. McMullen, Harold Gene: Enforcing the code of ethics of the education profession in Florida: A developmental study with implications for preservice teacher education (Ed.D. dissertation, University of Miami, 1970). *Dissertation Abstracts, 70,* 18166, 1970.

credit hours in professional ethics be required as a part of the certification regulations of every state.[9]

Greater attention to professional ethics is sorely needed in teacher education. How, then, should professional ethics be provided? Preservice teachers need to acquire a basic knowledge of professional ethics prior to student teaching, at some point in their early professional sequence of courses, in order to avert unethical behavior unknowingly and to get off to a good start in their teaching experiences. Inservice teachers could use materials suggested by Constans (though some materials he names are also appropriate for preservice teachers). Inservice teachers, however, can provide actual case studies for analysis; they should already have a basic grasp of professional codes and can therefore devote themselves to research, case studies, and a deeper analysis of ethical issues.

What form should professional ethics instruction take? A pervasive method would build ethical considerations into most all aspects of the professional sequence and would be the responsibility of each instructor. Though it would be admirable if all teacher educators were sensitive in their courses to such concerns, to leave it at this level may convey to students a general lack of concern for professional ethics, offer diffuse treatment, and erroneously expect instructors without expertise in the area to assume the task. A better approach is to offer a preservice course in professional ethics or not less than a substantial block of time (say, several units) in an existing 3-hour semester course (the latter approach is expedient where serious difficulties would arise in gaining approval for a new course). Coupled with formal instruction is on-the-job experience, first through student teaching and later full-time teaching, where case studies and job-related problems could be studied in seminars devoted to a cluster of cognate professional experiences.

What should be the content of these courses? The course for preservice teachers should thoroughly familiarize them with the NEA's Code and other pertinent codes of ethics. Questions by students should be elicited on the application of rules and standards of the various codes before carefully examining the principles that underlie the codes. Preservice teachers should be shown how professional ethics emerges from various conceptions of professionalism and what it means to become a professional educator. The seminar concurrent with student teaching, as already noted, would examine job-related problems and case studies; however, applicable principles would be delineated to give structure, meaning, and direction to the seminar.

The inservice seminar could begin with a similar, but more sophisticated, case-study approach and move to research reports and a deeper analysis of

---

9. Constans, Henry Philip: A method for development of an effective code of ethics for educators (Doctoral dissertation, University of Florida, 1962). *Dissertation Abstracts, 63*, 0266, 1962.

ethical issues. This deeper analysis might be similar to the types of analysis found in various chapters of this book; it might also include a comparative study of ethics in various professions. Of course knowledge of ethics and ethical behavior is a necessary but not a sufficient condition for professional ethical conduct; consequently, the educator needs to be observant of his or her actions in everyday situations, be motivated to act ethically, and have the discipline and persistence to act on one's ethical convictions. One way that this is accomplished is by cultivating good character traits that resist waywardness and wrongdoing.[10]

IMPLEMENTATION

How should violations of codes be reported? The AASA Code is clear on this matter; the NEA Code of Ethics separates implementation provisions from the Code and vests these functions with the NEA Review Board. The AAUP, on the other hand, leaves matters in the hands of the institutions themselves, even though the AAUP has not been averse to the establishment of standards of academic freedom and tenure, for which they have sought widespread adoption. Of course it may be said that in matters of professional ethics, each institution is in a better position to implement and enforce codes. But with academic freedom and tenure cases, the AAUP conducts investigations of institutions whenever believed warranted and, when found guilty, officially censures the institution or those responsible for the undesirable conditions. Another possible explanation is that in cases of academic freedom and tenure violations the AAUP's investigations serve to protect the faculty, whereas with violations of professional ethics their investigation (if they did begin conducting them) would more than likely aid the administration by uncovering and prosecuting faculty. Yet, even though the AAUP is a faculty organization, it would ultimately be in the interest of the Association to weed out unethical professors, even though ostensibly and in the short-run it may appear that the Association was working against some of its own members.

How swiftly should sanctions be applied in cases investigated? First a prima facie case needs to be made that professional ethics has likely been violated and an investigation is needed. Evidence pertinent to the case in question needs to be gathered by disinterested parties through a standing committee or other appointed body. Once the evidence is gathered, verified, and carefully discussed by the committee, a complete written report should be filed with the appropriate authorities. In other words, the investigating committee would not be the judicial body that will render a decision.

---

10. This is a complex problem that is discussed more fully in Straughan, Roger: *'I ought to but...' A Philosophical Approach to the Problem of Weakness of Will in Education.* Windsor, Berks., NFER–Nelson, 1982.

The teacher's rights to a hearing would need to be safeguarded because, whatever the final decision about the teacher's behavior, the outcome may likely be stigmatizing. Thus it is essential that the investigative body perform its task thoroughly in order to avoid issuing unsupportable accusations that could damage the teacher's professional reputation. Where charges are made against an educator, there should be adequate notice and a hearing before an impartial tribunal. The educator has the right to be represented by counsel, to present evidence and cross-examine witnesses, to receive a written copy of the findings, and have a right to appeal.

Effective implementation of an ethical code is facilitated by sound organization of the governing body and specific rules of behavior. An early comparative study of many different professions found that control was more effective in highly integrated organizations with well-developed machinery that employs a code comprised primarily of specific rules.[11] Also, according to Lieberman, a code should be clear enough to be applied in a variety of concrete cases, not impose unreasonable standards (i.e., supererogatory standards), should not regulate nonprofessional aspects of practitioners, it should not neglect any important ethical problem of the profession, and should maintain the concept of effective service as a primary consideration in all cases.[12] Many of these points are already familiar in light of our discussion in chapter two of the structure and functions of ethical codes. The point here is that the adequate implementation of ethical codes is obstructed by their internal deficiencies.

Should there be national norms or different professional norms between the states? Though each state may jealously guard its prerogative to establish professional licensing and certification standards, it would appear that national norms are called for in professional ethics, even though different education specialties may have their own codes (e.g., college professors, elementary and secondary teachers, administrators, guidance counselors, etc.). With certification, states that pay higher salaries may establish higher certification requirements; however, reciprocity in certification is the case today among a number of states. But whatever the merits of state licensing and certification, a national set of norms need to be established for professional ethics because the underlying principles are the same irrespective of which state one practices in, even though the application of the principles may vary.

The NEA rightly sought to develop a national code. The 1952 version of its code was adopted by 50 state associations, and the 1963 revision was

---

11. Landis, Benson Y.: *Professional Codes.* New York, Bureau of Publications, Teachers College, Columbia University, 1927, Introduction.

12. Lieberman, Myron: *Education as a Profession.* Englewood Cliffs, N.J., Prentice-Hall, 1956, pp. 417–18.

adopted by 56 state associations.[13] Many states in the past, however, developed their own codes rather than subscribe to the NEA Code. The NEA sought widespread participation and extended hearings in revising its code. Provision was made for its code to be reviewed continuously, amended or revised as appropriate, and reports made to the Representative Assembly in five-year cycles.[14] Thus some of the strengths of the NEA Code are that it is an evolving document subject to continuous review and enlisting widespread revision in its formulation, revision, and application.[14] The problem in achieving national norms is gaining the cooperation of various influential bodies and organizations at state and national levels. One organization that has not participated in developing and revising the NEA Code is the American Federation of Teachers (AFT). Until the AFT and other influential organizations are willing to participate with the NEA in this project, a truly nationwide code will not be put into effect.

As for college teaching, the AAUP or the college division of the NEA or AFT could attempt to initiate a code and involve related organizations and officials in the process. By first promoting the widespread recognition of a code and then involving the key organizations in its formulation, a nationwide code for college teachers could be developed.

A different type of implementation problem concerns the responsibility of professionals for their unethical members. Should sanctions be applied to professionals who observe misconduct among their colleagues but fail to report it? There is an unspoken code that one should not turn informer on one's colleagues, as this is a deceitful and insidious act, some believe, that may likely lead to the alienation of good working relationships with one's colleagues once they learn the identity of the informer. The attitude in this case is to leave the "dirty work" to authorities in the organization or to the public at large to detect and prosecute wrongdoers. A partial remedy for this attitude is to protect the identity of the informer, though it may not alleviate one's colleagues from thinking of the informer as treacherous and some informers from suffering guilt feelings or ambivalence.

A somewhat different situation has from time to time occurred in the federal government where employees informed their superiors or Congressional committees that their agencies were wasting millions of dollars. Some were fired; others were labelled troublemakers and then demoted. Some have had to wage lengthy and expensive court battles to regain their jobs. Of course not all charges by whistle blowers have proven to be accurate: some charges were unfounded; others have leveled misconduct charges after being

---

13. NEA: *Addresses and Proceedings*, Vol. 102, 1964, p. 97.

14. NEA: *Addresses and Proceedings*, Vol. 113, 1975, p. 122.

passed over for promotion; and still some have sought the status of whistle blower, as a defense against their own incompetence.[15]

Supervisors are responsible for conduct of subordinates carried out under the supervisor's orders, and are also responsible to oversee and take action against unethical behavior. Subordinates could also be held responsible for unequivocal behavior undertaken under the supervisor's direction, even though greater sanctions would be imposed on the supervisor.

Reporting of professional misconduct appears to be inadequate in a number of professions. In accounting, audit failures and management fraud during the mid-1970s prompted Congressional inquiry that led to the establishment of peer review, a special investigations committee, and a public oversight board. Audit failures are now infrequent, but when they do occur the profession seems averse to taking action. The American Institute of Certified Public Accountants has yet to expel a member as a result of peer review, and self-regulation has not led to revoking the license of any CPA.[16]

A study of physicians reported that physicians infrequently attended to unethical practices of colleagues; and when reports of such practices were made, they were rarely subject to regulation.[17] An ad hoc committee of the American Bar Association has found a similar problem among lawyers.[18]

The incidence of teachers and other educators reporting misconduct is not available, but the activities of some teacher organizations in prosecuting unethical behavior is partly available and will be presented in the next section. Public school teachers are supervised more than some other professionals (more than licensed physicians) but less than some professional or semi-professional groups (e.g., nurses). Teachers are more likely to be reported by nonprofessionals—students, parents, and other citizens—than some other professionals. A reason for this phenomenon is that laypersons believe (though sometimes erroneously) that they are knowledgeable about educational matters and are capable of evaluating professional competency and ethical behavior; whereas with lawyers and physicians, some people view their knowledge as esoteric and rely unquestioningly on the practitioner's authority. In any case, where reporting of unethical behavior by colleagues is infrequent or tacitly verboten among members, then an independent

15. For further discussion, see: Nader, Ralph, Petkas, Peter J., and Blackwell, Kate (Eds.): *Whistle Blowing.* New York, Grossman Publishers, 1972.

16. Auditing the auditors: Why Congress may tighten up. *Business Week,* No. 2820; 130, 135, December 12, 1983.

17. Freidson, Eliot: *Profession of Medicine: A Study of the Sociology of Applied Knowledge.* New York, Harper & Row, 1970, p. 158.

18. American Bar Association, Special Committee on Evaluation of Disciplinary Enforcement. *Problems and Recommendations in Disciplinary Enforcement.* Preliminary Draft. January 15, 1970. Chicago, American Bar Association, 1970.

standing committee comprised partly of laypersons should be established to facilitate the reporting of violations.

ENFORCEMENT

Of the different professions, law probably has the greatest control over its members' conduct, because the American Bar Association codes are adopted, with modifications, by courts or legislatures and thereby have legal force. In contrast, professional codes in education are enforced by school boards and administrative officials, NEA state affiliates, and the NEA. Occasionally courts are involved when aggrieved educators seek to overturn a decision.

Various types of sanctions may be imposed. The most widely found sanctions in the professions are the following: censure, professional ostracism and boycott, suspension or expulsion from professional society membership and withdrawal of other types of professional privileges, suits for malpractice, and suspension or revocation of license to practice.

Let us look in turn at each of these types of sanctions. Censure occurs as a result of an investigation when an authoritative body (school board, university board, the chief administrative official, an ad hoc investigative board, or professional organization) publicly expresses strong disapproval of the behavior of an individual or group of individuals. By going on record in voicing disapproval, it becomes a stern warning to the individual to either rectify his professional conduct or else face more serious charges. Thus censure has virtually the same effect as placing one on probationary status in matters of professional ethics.

Professional ostracism and boycott may occur when clients refuse to consult unethical professionals, and when other professionals refuse to refer clients to them. This type of sanction is more applicable to professions largely in private practice, as law and medicine, rather than education. Still, even if it is alleged that a teacher committed unethical acts but the charges never receive a formal hearing, the teacher may suffer ostracism from colleagues and parents, as well as a boycott by students. Thus it is important that administrators devise effective means for dispelling unfounded rumors and innuendos.

One's membership from a professional society may be suspended or revoked. The seriousness of this sanction depends upon the importance of the professional society in the profession in general, its significance to the individual who is disciplined, and the attendant adverse publicity from the sanctions. Thus a privilege to participate with fellow professionals and to enjoy the advantages of membership would be temporarily or permanently removed. Some professionals have certain unique privileges, such as hospital privileges for physicians, which can be revoked by the hospital board;

however, the revocation is not as serious as may be imagined, especially if the physician can gain privileges at another hospital. Some teachers do private tutoring and coaching; and since they are sometimes referred to parents from an approved list, the school administration can remove their names from the list. Any other privilege could be suspended or revoked, but there should be some relationship between the offense and the suspended privilege. For instance, repeated use of obscene language with young students may lead to the suspension of some tutoring opportunities but not necessarily suspension of membership in a professional organization.

Suits for malpractice are increasingly common in medical practice but rare in teaching. In two cases of nonfeasance (failure to educate properly) and in a third case of misfeasance (charges that the school failed to observe desirable professional practices), the courts ruled in favor of the schools.[19] Thus here we have an external rather than an internal sanction: namely a sanction imposed by laypersons rather than professionals. But if in the future judicial decisions go against teachers, one may see a situation in teaching analogous to what is happening in medical practice: many educators would likely refuse to staff high risk litigious job categories and those who continue to staff these positions would likely demand greater compensation and special privileges.

The suspension or revocation of professional licenses is a sanction employed in such professions as medicine and law; it is the most severe internal sanction that can be applied because it denies the privilege of practicing one's profession. Notice that the practice of a profession is a *privilege*, not a *right;* it is a privilege that can be suspended or revoked. Certification agencies have been zealous in assuring initial competency of teachers to practice, but less zealous in monitoring the continued competence of certificate holders—many states still provide lifetime certificates and no state has yet instituted a mandatory reassessment program. Most license laws make provisions for a formal hearing of serious charges; and if the licensee is found incompetent, negligent, or unfit to practice, the license may be suspended or revoked.[20] Figures are not available as to the percentage of all suspensions or revocations of certification on the ground of unethical professional conduct, but it is likely that most convictions are for incompetence.

Adherence to the Code of Ethics is a condition of membership in the NEA. A number of disciplinary cases have come before the NEA in the period, 1958 to the present. In 1962, one member was expelled for a felony

---

19. Fischer, Louis, Schimmel, David, and Kelly, Cynthia: *Teachers and the Law.* New York, Longman, 1981, p. 76.

20. Shimberg, Benjamin: Licensing and certification. *Encyclopedia of Educational Research* (Fifth Edition). New York, Free Press, 1982, vol. 3, pp. 1087–88.

conviction;[21] the Committee voted in 1964 to reprove one member, to formally censure another, to suspend a third for one year;[22] and it expelled a member in 1969, but at the request of a local and a state affiliate conducted a hearing to reconsider the case and reinstated the individual's membership in 1979.[23]

The NEA's National Commission for the Defense of Democracy Through Education and The National Commission on Professional Rights and Responsibilities investigated during the 1940s possible violations of the code of ethics.[24] Beginning in the 1950s the Committee on Professional Ethics was responsible for the development, dissemination, interpretation, and enforcement of the code of ethics. The Committee, as of July 1975, went out of existence and, in the new constitution, responsibility for enforcing the Code of Ethics was assigned to the NEA Review Board.[25] The NEA judicial powers are vested in the Review Board. Among the Board's powers are those of censure, suspension, or expulsion of a member for violating the Code of Ethics of the Education Profession or other sufficient cause; and to vacate censure, lift suspension, or reinstate a member.[26] The Review Board's policies for initiating proceedings against a member and conducting hearings scrupulously protects the member's rights to due process.[27]

In addition to soliciting widespread participation in revisions of the Code of Ethics and gaining widespread support from local and state affiliates, the NEA has sought collaboration with the AASA. The NEA attorney deemed the two codes of these organizations compatible. Because of different rationales, different procedures for enforcement are employed: the NEA utilizes a quasi-judicial procedure, while the AASA is patterned after the AMA and ABA, using an investigatory procedure on the order of a grand jury investigation. The latter procedure allows more confidentiality for the publicly sensitive role of the superintendent.[28]

In enforcing the NEA Code of Ethics, NaNakorn found that the 1963 version had inadequacies in the enforcement machinery and procedures as

21. NEA: *Addresses and Proceedings*, 1963, vol. 101, p. 311.

22. NEA: *Addresses and Proceedings*, 1964, vol. 102, pp. 279, 282, 285.

23. NEA Review Board: Decision No. 5, January 28, 1979.

24. Ethridge, Samuel B.: Letter to the author, January 25, 1984. Mr. Ethridge is Special Assistant to the Executive Director of the NEA.

25. Ethridge, Samuel B.: Letter to the author, December 23, 1983.

26. NEA *Governance Documents 1983–84:* Constitution: Article VII: Review Board. Washington, D.C., The Association, 1983.

27. For details about the procedures, see: NEA *Review Board Procedures.* Washington, D.C., The Association, 1980.

28. NEA: *Addresses and Proceedings*, 1970, vol. 108, p. 551.

well as in the interpretation and language of the Code.[29] The number of disciplinary cases turned up in our own investigation is amazingly small in view of the NEA's huge membership (currently over 1,700,000 members) and the Association's strong commitment over the years to the development, revision, dissemination, and interpretation of the Code. A salient reason for the low incidence of cases is that the Review Board itself does not initiate investigations of violations. What it does instead is to act once charges are filed with it by a governing body of an affiliate (of which the person charged is a member), by ten or more NEA members, or the Executive Director at the request of one or more NEA Members.[30] But this still fails to explain why more cases are not referred to the Review Board. Obviously NEA Members are averse to bringing charges or following-up on final action taken by school boards to report fellow members for unethical conduct. This failure to report, as noted earlier, is not unique to education.

But this is no ground for complacency among educators. It was shown in chapter one that education as a profession, in some of its other characteristics, is less professionally developed than law or medicine. These studies of enforcement, however, do point up the inadequacies of self-regulation and the need for greater participation by lay bodies.

It might be thought that the AASA, which has a more detailed code and elaborate levels of enforcement, would be more successful than the NEA in gaining compliance and disciplining members. Dexheimer found that the AASA Code of Ethics (adopted in 1962) had only five violations in the entire nation in 1967. His study sent questionnaires to 443 chief school administrators, containing anecdotal situations involving professional ethics. The responses, which were measured against the AASA Code of Ethics, raised doubts about relying on the Code, as more non-ethical than ethical responses were received. This indicates a discrepancy between acceptance of the Code (at least as measured by membership in the AASA) and adherence to the Code.[31]

A number of measures can be taken to improve the enforcement of ethical codes. First, a universal code, one accepted by all teachers, is still needed, despite great efforts by the NEA to bring this about. Of course administrators and other specialties need their own code but should also subscribe to the NEA Code (as the AASA superintendents have done) except when it is inapplicable to their specialty. One of the great stumbling blocks is that the AFT does not subscribe to the NEA Code and does not have a code of its

---

29. NaNakorn, Apirom: The code of ethics for the teaching profession: An analysis of problems (Ed.D. dissertation, Indiana University, 1965). *Dissertation Abstracts, 65,* 5302, 1965.

30. NEA *Review Board Procedures,* p. 9.

31. Dexheimer, Chester LeRoy: The administrative ethics of chief school administrators (Ed.D. dissertation, University of Rochester, 1969). *Dissertation Abstracts, 69,* 3670, 1969.

own. Since the AFT has over 500,000 members and is a strong national organization with many influential local affiliates, it is vital to solicit AFT cooperation in developing a universal code of ethics for the teaching profession. The NEA should also consult the AAUP to see the extent to which the present NEA Code is applicable to college professors.

Second, revocation of certification is a far more severe disciplinary sanction than loss of NEA membership and similar sanctions; therefore revocation should be employed more frequently and widely by State Departments of Education whenever the seriousness of the misconduct calls for strong discipline.

Just as the AAUP investigates violations of academic freedom and tenure, the NEA could initiate investigations of violations (rather than waiting for violations to be referred to the Board). Fourth, the NEA could encourage local and state affiliates to pursue cases vigorously and handle them more rigorously. Fifth, systematic preservice and inservice study of professional ethics should be promoted in teacher education programs. Sixth, greater on-the-job supervision by principals of probationary teachers is needed where particular attention is given to observing professional ethics in all one's dealings, using case studies and modeling behavior of exemplary ethical teachers. Finally, lay representation is needed in developing and revising ethical codes and to serve as members of disciplinary boards. Probably only when this measure is taken will education, as well as other professions, engage in widespread reporting and vigorous investigations of unethical behavior. The consistent application of the above proposals should greatly improve the implementation and enforcement of professional ethics in education.

Chapter Nine

REVIEW AND REASSESSMENT

Professional ethics in education covers a broad and expansive area and it may prove helpful now to take final retrospective and prospective views in order to highlight important points and pull together any loose strands. This chapter, therefore, reviews and reassesses some findings in previous chapters; it does this by first presenting the accomplishments and advancements in professional ethics and then delineating weaknesses remaining and proposals for bringing about desired changes.

ADVANCEMENTS IN PROFESSIONAL ETHICS

The NEA has been a leader in developing a code of ethics for the teaching profession, and in disseminating and interpreting it. It was indicated in the last chapter that the NEA Code of Ethics is an evolving document that has been revised many times in light of changing conditions and new professional problems. The revision process, though time-consuming and expensive, solicited widespread participation from members in state and local affiliates, all of which has led to a large pool of needed information from the field to base decisions and to elicit greater receptivity among teachers to the final document. The NEA has made a massive effort to disseminate the Code and has rendered valuable interpretations in difficult cases. The enforcement proceedings contain clearly demarcated regulations for hearings where the rights of the accused are duly protected.

Much progress has been made during the past 100 years in safeguarding academic freedom despite serious abuses during this century (notably, during World War I and the McCarthy period). The AAUP has exercised important leadership in this area by its vigorous defense of academic freedom and tenure principles; investigations and publication of violations has led to the revision of college and university policies and greater ethical behavior by administrators and boards of trustees. Also of importance are the AAUP's many important documents and policy statements, which have created a discernible position on the numerous ethical issues facing professors.

The AASA has formulated a code of ethics to govern the ethical professional behavior of school administrators and, as part of the code, has developed an elaborate structure of enforcement at national, state, and local levels. It clearly publicizes how these procedures are to be handled.

The protection of student rights and the freedom of students to learn has improved appreciably since the 1970s, as a consequence of court cases which upheld, among other provisions, due process for students. Teachers increasingly have recognized that the protection of academic freedom for faculty and the student's freedom to learn are complementary.

Much progress has been made since the 1960s in regulating research studies and providing ethical guidelines so that risks are reduced and benefits increased for the participants, researchers, and society at large. The initiative was first taken by the promulgation of the Nuremberg Code and was later pursued vigorously by agencies of the federal government.

In the area of recruitment in employment, civil rights legislation of the 1960s and Affirmative Action reduced discrimination in employment and helped overcome some past inequities. Debates over quotas for minority group hiring are still open to dispute; but the legal machinery is largely in place to abolish discrimination not only on grounds of race, religion, and ethnicity, but marital status and physical handicap as well.

In general, faculty rights are more widely recognized today as a result of court decisions and the militancy of unionized faculty associations. Thus faculty more freely dissent, engage in collective bargaining and strikes. Some difficult and perplexing ethical issues still persist in this area (as chapter six indicates).

The erstwhile narrow and restrictive community standards imposed upon teachers have abated and teachers in many communities are able to lead a normal life without continual surveillance. The AAUP, in documents since its Academic Freedom and Tenure Statement of 1940 (that in effect established a double standard for professors in the community), has mitigated and modified its provisions in recent statements and interpretations.

WEAKNESSES AND RECOMMENDED CHANGES

Teaching at the elementary and secondary level less fully meets professional criteria than does law and medicine. The development and enforcement of a code of ethics is one criterion of a profession; however, most criteria of a profession relate to competence rather than ethics. More fully developed professions, among other things, exercise greater control over standards of entrance and exclusion and make more autonomous decisions. One reason why it may be difficult to establish a strong relationship between the status of a profession and its handling of professional ethics has to do with the public's lack of knowledge about the amount of unethical behavior that remains unreported to authorities and the small number of professionals who are subject to disciplinary action.

Most professions, it has been estimated, show an ethical violation rate of 10–20 percent of its membership a year and educators are probably no exception.[1] Perhaps the public underestimates the violation rate in some professions and overestimates it in business. In a Gallup Organization poll, 49 percent of the public think that ethical standards in business have declined in the past decade, while only 9 percent believe it has risen.[2] In contrast, only 23 percent of business executives believe that business ethics have declined in the past decade, while 31 percent think it has risen. Perhaps workers know something about themselves of which executives are not entirely cognizant: 40 percent said they had snitched supplies from work and taken them home and 31 percent reported that they had called in sick when they were not ill. In other studies, it is estimated that employees steal from $40 billion to $100 billion from their companies each year, and more than 30 percent of all business failures are caused by internal theft.[3] This serious problem could be largely prevented, according to experts, by tightening inventory controls and hiring procedures.

Looking at the weaknesses of specific codes of ethics, the AAUP Statement of Professional Ethics can be criticized for its brevity, its omission of important concerns (e.g., nepotism, outside employment, etc.) by leaving their treatment for other documents; the Statement also makes no provision for implementation and turns over enforcement to institutional officials rather than empowering the Association to conduct investigations. The AAUP should attempt to rectify these shortcomings; it should bring together in one document all areas of professional ethics (leaving elaboration to the original documents), widely disseminate its new document, and conduct hearings whenever the Statement is violated by one of its members. Since a majority of professors are not AAUP members, enforcement in these cases would rest at the institutional level (since the institutions are unlikely to delegate this responsibility to the AAUP) and with other associations that subscribe to the AAUP Statement.

The NEA Code has stated 16 rules negatively, rather than positively. Positive statements, however, are better motivating devices; in contrast, negative statements may be able to specify and circumscribe behavior more carefully; nevertheless, positive statements are generally preferable. Another problem is that the latest revision of the NEA Code has inexplicably omitted important areas covered in earlier versions of the Code (e.g., relations with parents). The AFT also needs to collaborate with the NEA on professional ethics.

---

1. *Encyclopedia of Education*, s.v. "Code of Ethics."

2. Executives and general public say ethical behavior is declining in the U.S. *The Wall Street Journal, 72,* 25, 41, October 31, 1983.

3. Stealing from the boss. *Newsweek, 102,* 78, December 26, 1983.

In terms of the contents of the various codes, one is not always clear who the principal clients may be; although it may be assumed that the client is the student, service to the profession, school board, and the public may also be plausible candidates as clients. Another problem is that little has been done with the justification of professional ethics and ethical codes in education (in contrast to the important and extensive studies lately in medical ethics). This deficiency causes insufficient warrant for code provisions and a lack of understanding as to how codes can best be grounded.

Far too little attention has been given to professional ethics in teacher education. In contrast, since the Watergate years, 322 business ethics courses have been added nationwide to the business curriculum in higher education.[4] In sharp contrast, few teacher education programs provide a systematic study of professional ethics, even though student teachers and beginning full-time teachers will be held fully accountable for observing ethical behavior.

All three codes studied earlier have some problems with enforcement. The problem may lie partly with the sacrosanct belief in professional autonomy. The greater autonomy of various professions, which has advantages in decision-making and controlling the profession by its members, has not generally been advantageous in professional ethics because far too few cases have been reported and even fewer have been prosecuted. Because enforcement has been unsatisfactory for many years and since there is no evidence that it will voluntarily be improved by professionals themselves, greater lay participation is needed in regulating and enforcing professional ethics. Both professionals and nonprofessionals should participate and each group should select their own representatives. Services professionals provide are greatly in the public interest; therefore to protect this interest, nonprofessionals should have full representation in deliberation and decision making.

In terms of testing and evaluation, more questions about teacher competence, rather than professional ethics, are raised; the ethical side, however, has been neglected and teachers need to sensitize themselves to these issues and relationships. As for student dishonesty on tests, part of the problem is the faculty's dereliction of duty: few instructors check out even a representative portion of sources, citations, and written materials submitted by students, and many faculty members are unwilling to proctor examinations rigorously. By adopting a theory of moral development, teachers may be better able to understand, anticipate, and interpret problems of student honesty.

More aggressive policies are needed to root out plagiarism, fraud, and

---

4. Board room, classroom exploring business ethics. *The Christian Science Monitor, 75,* 15–16, October 25, 1983.

other types of misconduct in research. There should be closer supervision of subordinates' research and less tolerance of subtle forms of plagiarism as well as a need for universities to take steps to protect researchers accused of dishonest acts. Here, as in other areas, the reluctance to bring charges against colleagues permits many violations to go unreported.

Periods of retrenchment pose dangers to the integrity of the faculty and the curriculum by possible expediency of administrators, boards, and legislators. Thus faculty may wish to oppose tenure quotas and term tenure. Faculty members need to show that when they defend a certain tenure plan, they not only are pursuing their professional self-interest but are ultimately acting to promote the good of the university; this could be accomplished by showing that, despite contrary claims of some critics, tenure helps ensure academic freedom. As for retrenchment, guidelines need to be developed jointly by faculty and administrators prior to periods of financial exigency so as to avert abuses, accept responsibility for joint planning and decisions, develop an orderly and rational procedure for handling retrenchment, and make certain that any declared emergency is bona fide and demonstrable and not a guise for eliminating unpopular programs or unpopular faculty members.

Thus, despite the work that remains to be done, one can take pride in the many solid accomplishments in professional ethics in education. The unfinished tasks can be accomplished by mobilizing the most influential organizations and leaders who in turn will seek the cooperation of all educators. By doing so educators will thereby assure the dignity of their profession, mutual trust, cooperation, and public support.

APPENDIX

CODE OF ETHICS OF THE EDUCATION PROFESSION

ADOPTED BY THE 1975 NEA REPRESENTATIVE ASSEMBLY

Preamble

The educator, believing in the worth and dignity of each human being, recognizes the supreme importance of the pursuit of truth, devotion to excellence, and the nurture of democratic principles. Essential to these goals is the protection of freedom to learn and to teach and the guarantee of equal educational opportunity for all. The educator accepts the responsibility to adhere to the highest ethical standards.

The educator recognizes the magnitude of the responsibility inherent in the teaching process. The desire for the respect and confidence of one's colleagues, of students, of parents, and of the members of the community provides the incentive to attain and maintain the highest possible degree of ethical conduct. The Code of Ethics of the Education Profession indicates the aspiration of all educators and provides standards by which to judge conduct.

The remedies specified by the NEA and/or its affiliates for the violation of any provision of this Code shall be exclusive and no such provision shall be enforceable in any form other than one specifically designated by the NEA or its affiliates.

Principle I—Commitment to the Student

The educator strives to help each student realize his or her potential as a worthy and effective member of society. The educator therefore works to stimulate the spirit of inquiry, the acquisition of knowledge and understanding, and the thoughtful formulation of worthy goals.

In fulfillment of the obligation to the student, the educator—

1. Shall not unreasonably restrain the student from independent action in the pursuit of learning.
2. Shall not unreasonably deny the student access to varying points of view.
3. Shall not deliberately suppress or distort subject matter relevant to the student's progress.
4. Shall make reasonable effort to protect the student from conditions harmful to learning or to health and safety.
5. Shall not intentionally expose the student to embarrassment or disparagement.

6. Shall not on the basis of race, color, creed, sex, national origin, marital status, political or religious beliefs, family, social or cultural background, or sexual orientation, unfairly:
   a. Exclude any student from participation in any program;
   b. Deny benefits to any student;
   c. Grant any advantage to any student.
7. Shall not use professional relationships with students for private advantage.
8. Shall not disclose information about students obtained in the course of professional service, unless disclosure serves a compelling professional purpose or is required by law.

Principle II—Commitment to the Profession

The education profession is vested by the public with a trust and responsibility requiring the highest ideals of professional service.

In the belief that the quality of the services of the education profession directly influences the nation and its citizens, the educator shall exert every effort to raise professional standards, to promote a climate that encourages the exercise of professional judgment, to achieve conditions which attract persons worthy of the trust to careers in education, and to assist in preventing the practice of the profession by unqualified persons.

In fulfillment of the obligation to the profession, the educator—

1. Shall not in an application for a professional position deliberately make a false statement or fail to disclose a material fact related to competency and qualifications.
2. Shall not misrepresent his/her professional qualifications.
3. Shall not assist entry into the profession of a person known to be unqualified in respect to character, education, or other relevant attribute.
4. Shall not knowingly make a false statement concerning the qualifications of a candidate for a professional position.
5. Shall not assist a noneducator in the unauthorized practice of teaching.
6. Shall not disclose information about colleagues obtained in the course of professional service unless disclosure serves a compelling professional purpose or is required by law.
7. Shall not knowingly make false or malicious statements about a colleague.
8. Shall not accept any gratuity, gift, or favor that might impair or appear to influence professional decisions or actions.

STATEMENT ON PROFESSIONAL ETHICS

The Statement on Professional Ethics was approved by the Council of the American Association of University Professors in April, 1966, and endorsed by the Fifty-second Annual Meeting as Association policy.

Introduction

From its inception, the American Association of University Professors has recognized that membership in the academic profession carries with it special responsibilities. The Association has consistently affirmed these responsibilities in major policy statements, providing guidance to the professor in his utterances as a citizen, in the exercise of his responsibilities to students, and in his conduct when resigning from his institution or when undertaking government-sponsored research.[1] The *Statement on Professional Ethics* that follows, necessarily presented in terms of the ideal, sets forth those general standards that serve as a reminder of the variety of obligations assumed by all members of the profession. For the purpose of more detailed guidance, the Association, through its Committee B on Professional Ethics, intends to issue from time to time supplemental statements on specific problems.

In the enforcement of ethical standards, the academic profession differs from those of law and medicine, whose associations act to assure the integrity of members engaged in private practice. In the academic profession the individual institution of higher learning provides this assurance and so should normally handle questions concerning propriety of conduct within its own framework by reference to a faculty group. The Association supports such local action and stands ready, through the General Secretary and Committee B, to counsel with any faculty member or administrator concerning questions of professional ethics and to inquire into complaints when local consideration is impossible or inappropriate. If the alleged offense is deemed sufficiently serious to raise the possibility of dismissal, the procedures should be in accordance with the 1940 *Statement of Principles on Academic Freedom and Tenure* and the 1958 *Statement on Procedural Standards in Faculty Dismissal Proceedings.*

The Statement

I. The professor, guided by a deep conviction of the worth and dignity of the advancement of knowledge, recognizes the special responsibilities placed upon him. His primary responsi-

---

[1]1964 Committee A Statement on Extra-Mural Utterances (Clarification of sec. 1c of the 1940 *Statement of Principles on Academic Freedom and Tenure*)

1968 *Joint Statement on Rights and Freedoms of Students*

1961 *Statement on Recruitment and Resignation of Faculty Members*

1964 *On Preventing Conflicts of Interest in Government-Sponsored Research*

1966 *Statement on Government of Colleges and Universities*

bility to his subject is to seek and to state the truth as he sees it. To this end he devotes his energies to developing and improving his scholarly competence. He accepts the obligation to exercise critical self-discipline and judgment in using, extending, and transmitting knowledge. He practices intellectual honesty. Although he may follow subsidiary interests, these interests must never seriously hamper or compromise his freedom of inquiry.

II. As a teacher, the professor encourages the free pursuit of learning in his students. He holds before them the best scholarly standards of his discipline. He demonstrates respect for the student as an individual, and adheres to his proper role as intellectual guide and counselor. He makes every reasonable effort to foster honest academic conduct and to assure that his evaluation of students reflects their true merit. He respects the confidential nature of the relationship between professor and student. He avoids any exploitation of students for his private advantage and acknowledges significant assistance from them. He protects their academic freedom.

III. As a colleague, the professor has obligations that derive from common membership in the community of scholars. He respects and defends the free inquiry of his associates. In the exchange of criticism and ideas he shows due respect for the opinions of others. He acknowledges his academic debts and strives to be objective in his professional judgment of colleagues. He accepts his share of faculty responsibilities for the governance of his institution.

IV. As a member of his institution, the professor seeks above all to be an effective teacher and scholar. Although he observes the stated regulations of the institution, provided they do not contravene academic freedom, he maintains his right to criticize and seek revision. He determines the amount and character of the work he does outside his institution with due regard to his paramount responsibilities within it. When considering the interruption or termination of his service, he recognizes the effect of his decision upon the program of the institution and gives due notice of his intentions.

V. As a member of his community, the professor has the rights and obligations of any citizen. He measures the urgency of these obligations in the light of his responsibilities to his subject, to his students, to his profession, and to his institution. When he speaks or acts as a private person he avoids creating the impression that he speaks or acts for his college or university. As a citizen engaged in a profession that depends upon freedom for its health and integrity, the professor has a particular obligation to promote conditions of free inquiry and to further public understanding of academic freedom.

INDEX